Ronald

IN a
BaRLEY
FiELD

IN a
BARLEY
FIELD

BY J. VERNON McGEE

A Division of G/L Publications
Glendale, California, U.S.A.

Published by
Regal Books Division, G/L Publications
Glendale, California, U.S.A.
Library of Congress Catalog Card No. 68-22387

Contents

PREFACE

The subject of redemption has been studied and interpreted continuously from the days of Paul, and it is not possible to make any startling new contribution to so rich a theme as this. Theories of redemption have sprung up like mushrooms in every age. Another word on this subject can but increase the babel of voices. However, there has been one aspect of the topic that has been almost entirely neglected. That is the "kinsman-redeemer" feature. As the Book of Ruth is the only historical illustration in the Bible of the Hebrew *goel*, the Book of Ruth makes a real contribution to this already overcrowded field. The conflicting theories of redemption would have been delivered from extreme and radical positions if this little brochure had been given the place it rightly deserves. The law of Moses excluded the Moabitess, and the theories of men have excluded the book which bears her name.

There has been no attempt to exhaust the subject of redemption, but rather to highlight the relationship of the Book of Ruth to redemption. Redemption is told in the language of romance in this story of Ruth. The terms of the marketplace, the clink of silver on the counter and the shoptalk of buying and selling are entirely omitted from its simple pages. The language of life, love and light is spoken. This is the language understood by simple, sinful folk.

CHAPTER 1

A Person or a Thing

The Book of Ruth has been recognized as a literary gem in most unexpected quarters. It is reported that Dr. Samuel Johnson, the literary giant of the eighteenth century, made a copy of the Book of Ruth and read it before a London club as a production he had recently read. The club, thinking it was a modern composition, was loud and unanimous in its praise of the manuscript. Then Dr. Johnson informed them that it was taken from a book which they all rejected—the Bible.

The beauty and excellence of this story cannot escape the most casual reader. This little brochure of beauty records the love story of the maid from Moab. It reveals the power of passionate and pure love. It tells, first of all, the strong attachment of Ruth to her mother-in-law, "for love is strong as death." It records a romance that triumphed over racial and religious barriers, and of two hearts that were joined together "with bands of love." The Book of Ruth is a laboratory demonstration that "the greatest of these is love."

The remarkable feature about the entire book is that the word "love" is entirely omitted from the narrative. It does not occur even once. This is altogether amazing when it is recognized that our modern age uses the term "love" frequently in all of its literature. Every novel, every song and every play abounds with a superfluity *ad nauseam* of this word. It is certainly overworked in an age that boasts of its sophisticated genius. Perhaps the literary lights today might learn from this love story that the most ardent passion and the deepest devotion do not require the "raven-like" repetition of this much abused word. The most precious object will become soiled by much handling, and love will become commonplace by constant use.

What beautiful restraint is exercised in this simple story, yet what soul-stirring passion of a noble and strong man and a beautiful and queenly woman is portrayed for us. On the human plane, this book tells of the sanctity of domestic life and the holiness of marital love. It lifts marriage to a very high position. It exalts true manhood and virtuous womanhood. It gives the lie to the modern triangle and it condemns the divorce evil. The Book of Ruth blesses the marriage vow. It sets before the reader the high ideals of wedlock in the time of Samson.

The Bible has been labeled and libeled by some of its critics as a man's book in which woman is neglected or ignored. Like most criticism, this caricature of the Bible is built upon a false assumption. The Book of Ruth contributes to the destruction of this false notion. There are two books in the Bible that bear the name of women. They tell the heart-story of two noble women. These are the Books of Ruth and Esther. Ruth tells the story of a Gentile girl who married an Israelite; Esther tells the story of a Jewish maiden who married a Gentile. In the New Testament there is one book written to a woman. It is the Second Epistle of John which is addressed "unto the elect lady and her children." Woman's place is prominent in the Bible and she is not ignored. The Book of Ruth tells the life story of a Gentile girl who "did build the house of Israel," and of one who was "famous in Bethlehem." The Book of Ruth is essentially a woman's story, and God has set his seal of approval upon it by its inclusion in the divine library.

The Jews ascribed an unusual importance to this book. In the national life of Israel it figured prominently. During the Feast of Pentecost, it was read. Dr. Gaebelein places it with four other books that were read during the five great feasts of the Jews. He says: "Five books are called by the Jews 'Megilloth' and are read by them at different feasts commemorating past events. The Song of Solomon is read during Passover; Ruth at Pentecost; Lamentations on the ninth day of the month Ab in memory of the destruction of Jerusalem; Ecclesiastes is read during the Feast of Tabernacles and Esther they read when they celebrate Purim."

This seemingly uneventful story of an insignificant

3

family during the days of national decline in Israel was given a place of unusual importance. It would appear on first examination that its position was out of all proportion to the merits of the story. On more careful consideration, this book looms up on the skyline of Scripture as a book of skyscraper significance. The very fact that it was read on the Day of Pentecost will prove suggestive to the Christian. Pentecost suggests the first birthday of the Church. Pentecost marks the "Bethlehem of the Holy Spirit," for he came on that day to indwell flesh. "Know ye not that your body is the temple of the Holy Ghost which is in you" (I Corinthians 6:19)?

Pentecost is the line of demarcation between law and grace. It marks the ending of the age of law and the beginning of the age of grace. The Book of Ruth tells the story of grace. It is pure grace from beginning to end. It tells the story of how a Gentile girl, whom the law condemned, was brought under the wings of the Lord God of Israel. How could she enter when the law said, "An Ammonite or Moabite shall not enter into the congregation of the Lord" (Deuteronomy 23:3)? Ruth was brought all the way in and every step of the way by grace. She believed Boaz, and he brought her into his heart and home. By grace was she saved through faith.

This story comes from the period of the judges. It was a time of political decay, moral degradation and spiritual degeneration. The recorded events occurred during the time of the judges, a period which began after the death of Joshua and continued to the time of Samuel. This decadent era extended over a period of about four hundred

4

years. In many respects these were the darkest days in the history of Israel. The Israelites had been redeemed from Egypt by blood, brought safely through the wilderness by power, and delivered to the "land of promise" personally by God. It would appear that with such a propitious background, they were on the threshold of great blessing and much prosperity. Certainly such an auspicious entrance afforded high expectations of the future. Their tragic failure makes the gloom all the more impressive. The story of Ruth stands in bright bas-relief by contrast with the dark ages of the judges.

The Book of Ruth is unique in that here there is set before the reader the only example in the Bible of the kinsman-redeemer at work. Herein is a detailed account of the Hebrew *goel* functioning in his full capacity. There could be no redemption for either property or the individual without the person and presence of a kinsman-redeemer. Unless the work of the kinsman-redeemer is adequately apprehended, there cannot be a comprehension of the work of redemption. Redemption requires a kinsman-redeemer.

Boaz furnishes us with a miniature figure of the Lord Jesus Christ as the Redeemer. Boaz is the type, and Christ is the antitype. A full treatment of the theme of redemption necessitates a careful consideration of the Book of Ruth. This, however, has been neglected by many of the reputable writers on the theme of redemption. Jonathan Edwards in the *History of Redemption*, Stuart Robinson in the *Discourse of Redemption*, and Sir Robert Anderson in *For Us Men* entirely omit any reference to the Book of Ruth. This seems all the more remarkable as each one of these writers traces the history of redemption through the Old Testament, paying particular attention to the figures and types.

As a result of this method of writing, redemption has come to mean a cold business transaction, devoid of the personal element. God did not buy man in the slave market of sin as a chattel is bought and sold. Redemption is not the story of a sharp trader who made a profitable investment in the marts of trade. No, a thousand times no! Redemption is the love story of a kinsman who did not count the cost nor figure up the profit and loss but for joy paid an exorbitant price for one that he loved. The Book of Ruth declares that redemption is not a business transaction but a love affair. The personal element must not be withdrawn from the doctrine of redemption, or the most vital part will be sacrificed.

The presence of the Book of Ruth in the Old Testament is justified by a fourfold purpose. Any one of these purposes furnishes a worthy motive for including it in the canon of Scripture. They are given in the reverse order of their importance: namely, (1) the historical purpose; (2) the dispensational purpose; (3) the genealogical purpose; and (4) the doctrinal purpose.

CHAPTER 2

Little Bethlehem

The record of one small family is contained in the Book of Ruth, and certainly their story is not spectacular. However, it does throw a most important sidelight upon the times of the judges. The period of the judges, as has been stated previously, was a day of decline and decay. "Ichabod" was written over this phase of the history of Israel. There is a proverb that identifies this time of the judges. It is, "Righteousness exalteth a nation: but sin is a reproach to any people" (Proverbs 14:34).

The time of the judges proved the accuracy of that statement. That proverb furnishes a philosophy of history for all nations at all times. Every nation in antiquity demonstrated the truth of that statement. The silent ruins and dead ashes of destroyed civilizations bear silent but eloquent testimony to this profound truth. The time of the judges is but a mere page out of a long list. Every nation that has followed righteousness has been exalted. Every nation that has taken the well-beaten path of sin has finally gone down into the dust of oblivion, fit only for the spade of the archaeologist. Israel took the familiar path of sin and reproach, and ignominy came upon them like an avalanche. War and long periods of servitude punctuated this period indelibly. Faithlessness to God and immorality characterized this age. However, there were rare instances of those in the nation who remained true to the God of Abraham, Isaac and Jacob. These were fit vessels with which he worked.

The incidents in Ruth deal with some who remained true to God. Here we have recorded life at its best during that evil day. Some have considered the Book of Ruth an appendix to the Book of Judges. MacNaughton described it as "a kind of appendix to the Book of Judges." The Book of Ruth furnishes us with very important clues to the times of the judges by way of contrast, but this does not necessitate considering it as a part of the Book of Judges. The Book of Ruth stands on its own foundation. It shows that in the darkest days, God was working out his purposes in the lives of individuals who were rightly related to him. God is always interested in the private affairs of humble folk, and this book tells how he moved in their lives. God touched the simple lives of these unknown village folk and made them sublime. The Book of Ruth is a pearl in the swine pen of the judges. When God touched the lives of these pastoral people, he brought them into the light of his program for eternity.

We are accustomed to making a distinction between the sacred and profane. In a very real way that is a false delineation. We automatically classify some things as sacred and some as secular. Before God all life is sacred. Even the details of life and the monotonous duties of the day are not profane, Washing dishes, gleaning wheat, standing at the workbench, sitting in the office and digging a ditch are all sacred when lived in the presence of God. The Christian is called upon to live his entire life unto the Lord. "Whether therefore ye eat, or drink, or whatsoever ye do, do all to the glory of God" (I Corinthians 10:31).

The historical significance of this book is clearly apparent when considered in relation to the little town of Bethlehem. It is the story in the Book of Ruth that lifts Bethlehem out of "the thousands of Judah," and identifies it as the city of David. It rescues Bethlehem from oblivion. The story of the birth of Christ in Bethlehem loses much of its meaning unless it is seen in the light of the Book of Ruth.

The question is sometimes asked: Why was Bethlehem chosen as the birthplace of Jesus? The Book of Ruth answers that question. The first time that the mention of Bethlehem occurs in Scripture is not in connection with this story, but with an incident which took place before Israel became a nation in Egypt. It was in connection with the birth of Benjamin and the death of Rachel. Benjamin was born in Bethlehem. It was not the birth of Benjamin that gave prominence to this place but the birth of Another. However, it is interesting to note in passing that a birth was the first event to call attention to this city. In giving birth to Benjamin, Rachel sacrificed her life and was buried there. "And Rachel died, and was buried in the way to Ephrath, which is Bethlehem" (Genesis 35:19). We also learn that the original name of Bethlehem was Ephrath, a name that was associated with it in the great prophecy in Micah. Jacob never forgot Bethlehem out of all the places that he had visited. When he was an old man and about to die in Egypt, he remembered Bethlehem as the place where he had buried his beautiful Rachel. "And as for me, when I came from Padan, Rachel died by me in the land of Canaan in the way, when yet there was but a little way to come unto Ephrath: and I buried her there in the way of Ephrath; the same as Bethlehem" (Genesis 48:7). Jacob remembered Bethlehem because of a death. The world remembers Bethlehem because of a birth.

There is not another important reference to Bethlehem until we come to the Book of Ruth. Ibzan, one of the judges, was born there, but only casual mention is made of the fact. All the events of importance in the Book of Ruth center around Bethlehem. The family of Elimelech came from Bethlehem. Naomi returned with Ruth to Bethlehem. Boaz lived at Bethlehem. Ruth was redeemed at Bethlehem. She was wed to Boaz at Bethlehem. Her son, Obed, was born at Bethlehem. Ruth lived the remainder of her life at Bethlehem; and we are to infer that she died and was buried at Bethlehem.

It is the story in the Book of Ruth that brought Bethlehem into the family of David. Had not the events of this story taken place, David would never have been born in Bethlehem and likewise Christ would never have been born there. In other words, it was the coming of Ruth from Moab that foreshadowed the coming of Christ to Bethlehem. When the Bible record is examined as a whole, then the Book of Ruth is seen in its true relationship. It is one of the most important cogs in the wheel of God's plan.

It is not strange to hear a prophet announce that the Messiah, who was to sit on David's throne and be David's son, was to be born in Bethlehem. It would have been strange had he spoken otherwise. Three hundred years after David, the prophet of God announced that Bethlehem would be the birthplace of the Messiah, which forever established this place as the most famous spot to the world, with the exception of Jerusalem. "But thou, Bethlehem Ephratah, though thou be little among the thousands of Judah, yet out of thee shall he come forth unto me that is to be ruler in Israel; whose goings forth have been from of old, from everlasting" (Micah 5:2).

The amazing thing about this prophecy is not that Bethlehem was chosen as the place of birth, for the Book of Ruth identified it, but that Bethlehem was the spot where the Saviour was born. This prophecy was uttered over seven hundred years before the event actually took place. During that time the house of David was taken from the throne, the city of Jerusalem was demolished, and the

11

nation was carried away captive to a strange land. In the face of these circumstances, it made the fulfillment of this an unlikelihood. "When the fulness of the time was come, God sent forth his Son," but the mother of the child dwelt in Nazareth. There was no earthly reason why she should go to Bethlehem. The Davidic family were now peasants and Bethlehem was no longer the place of refuge for them. How could Jesus be born in Bethlehem?

God was moving. When Caesar Augustus affixed his seal to a tax bill, calling upon the Roman world for a new assessment to keep its legions marching upon the Roman roads to the far-flung corners of its great empire, little did he realize that he was but a puppet in the hands of an omnipotent God. He was carrying out the decree of a power greater than he. Luke, with a historian's pen, wrote, "And it came to pass in those days, that there went out a decree from Caesar Augustus, that all the world should be taxed" (Luke 2:1). This taxing had repercussions throughout the empire. Out in the hinterlands of a small country in the out-of-the-way village of Nazareth some descendants of Boaz and Ruth started on a long trek toward Bethlehem that the Word of God might be literally fulfilled. Let Luke again take up the historian's pen and write: "And Joseph also went up from Galilee, out of the city of Nazareth, into Judea, unto the city of David, which is called Bethlehem; (because he was of the house and lineage of David:) to be taxed with Mary his espoused wife, being great with child. And so it was, that, while they were there, the days were accomplished that she should be delivered. And she brought forth her firstborn son, and wrapped him in swaddling clothes, and laid him in a manger; because there was no room for them in the inn" (Luke 2:4-7).

The ancestral home of David was not there to receive them. The redeemed property of Boaz was no longer theirs. They sought refuge with the beasts of the field, but God's Word was carried out to the letter, and the Book of Ruth was justified and found its proper place in the program of God.

> "O little town of Bethlehem!
>   How still we see thee lie,
> Above thy deep and dreamless sleep,
>   The silent stars go by;
> Yet in thy dark streets shineth
>   The everlasting Light,
> The hopes and fears of all the years
>   Are met in thee tonight."

CHAPTER 3

A Beautiful Picture

The dispensational aspect of the Book of Ruth bulks large to many Bible students. In fact, some see this as the supreme objective. In the family of Elimelech, departing from the land of Israel to the land of Moab, many see a picture of Israel, absent from the land of Canaan and scattered throughout the world. The Gentile girl is brought into the place of blessing during this interval. The Church today occupies the place of blessing, and corresponds to the Gentile. Someday the Church will be united to Christ Jesus who is greater than Boaz. In that day the Jew will return to the land of promise and blessing will ensue.

Even the position of the book in the Old Testament canon is suggestive to some Bible teachers. It is not accidental that the Book of Ruth appears after

Judges and before First Samuel. Judges tells the story of the failure of the theocracy under the Mosaic system, and First Samuel tells of the setting up of the monarchy. Between the failure and rejection and the kingdom, there occurs Ruth, the Gentile bride. Between the rejection of the nation of Israel and the setting up of the kingdom on the earth, there is found the Church, the bride of the Lamb.

There is another phase in this category that is suggestive. Here we find God's salvation going forth to the Gentiles in spite of the failure of Israel. Dispensationally, this little book sets forth the age of grace. It tells how the lowly foreigner, ostracized by the law of Moses, found redemptive rest in Boaz. He exercised grace in her behalf and thereby brought her under the protection of his name and home. Ruth is thought by many to be a type of the Church and Boaz a type of Christ. There is a beautiful analogy here that is worthy of much thought; but there is a real danger of overemphasizing this interpretation.

There are seven marriage types in the Old Testament which depict some phase of the relationship that exists between Christ and the Church. These are: Adam and Eve, Isaac and Rebekah, Joseph and Asenath, Moses and Zipporah, Ruth and Boaz, David and Abigail, and Solomon and the shepherdess in the Song of Solomon. Ruth and Boaz set before us the grace that exists between Christ and his Church. There is no lovelier figure used to describe the relationship between Christ and the Church than that of bridegroom and bride. There is no

15

more beautiful type in the Old Testament than Boaz and Ruth as they represent grace. We hesitate to develop this purpose of the Book of Ruth for fear of wandering off into the field of speculation. This is a fruitful study, pregnant with deep spiritual meaning, but we shall leave it for wiser heads and deeper hearts to develop.

CHAPTER 4

Getting the Family Straight

The inadequacy of a brief definition as to the purpose of the Bible is self-evident, but these brief statements sometimes contain pertinent facts. This is true in the following statements of purpose of the Old Testament: The purpose of the Old Testament is to furnish a reliable genealogy of the Lord Jesus Christ. Certainly there needs to be no insistence on the fact that the line which leads to Christ from Adam is the one which is persistently followed in Scripture; and the story of that family is recorded in detail, while mere mention is made of more prominent personalities of that day.

The Book of Genesis has as its primary purpose the listing of the generations of a family. Eleven generations are enumerated. The method adopted by the Divine Author is to record all the offspring

17

of the chosen line, and then to omit a detailed account of the rejected line and give a brief summary of the reasons for the omission. The record of the chosen line is resumed, and the elect offspring is described and his story given in detail (*e.g.*, Abraham had other children besides Isaac, but only the line of Isaac is followed through the Bible. Isaac had another son besides Jacob, but only Jacob's line is given). The story of the chosen line is the theme of Scripture. Israel was in fact an elect nation.

This being true, the Book of Ruth furnishes the most important link in the Old Testament. It connects David with the tribe of Judah. By so doing, it produces a homogeneous character to the Old Testament. Under these circumstances, the genealogical purpose makes the Book of Ruth one of the most essential to the Old Testament canon. The older theologians called attention to this. However, there are those who not only minimize this but actually reject it. MacNaughton says:

"Their (the older theologians) most specious contention was that the Holy Spirit had so ordered it should be there, in order that we might have some account of an ancestress of the Messiah."

The Book of Ruth supplies data that is essential to the genealogy of the chosen line. This cannot be discounted and a casual perusal shows that the presentation of a genealogy is the evident intent of the writer. Kiel and Delitzsch recognize this and call particular attention to it: "In this conclusion the meaning and tendency of the whole narrative is brought clearly to light. The genealogical proof of the descent of David from Pharez through Boaz and the Moabitess Ruth (chapter 4:18-22) forms not only the end, but the starting point, of the history contained in the book."

Auberlen expressed the importance of the genealogical purpose of Ruth in even stronger terms. "The Book of Ruth contains, as it were, the inner side, the spiritually moral background of the genealogies which play so significant a part even in the Israelitish antiquity."

James Morison is alarmed that there were many who not only considered the genealogical purpose to be the primary one, but actually thought it the only purpose for the existence of the book in the Scripture. He wrote: "Many have supposed that the true *raison d'être* of the book is a matter of genealogy . . . Yet it seems preposterous to assume that the whole graphic story of Ruth was composed simply in consequence of this genealogical interest."

We shall not assume here that the only purpose of the Book of Ruth is to furnish a genealogy, but contrariwise, we shall not take the position that the purpose is not to give us a genealogy. There is overwhelming evidence that this was one of the major motives. We can say with Kiel and Delitzsch: "The last words of verse 17, 'he is the father of Jesse, the father of David,' show the object which the author had in view in writing down these events, or composing the book itself. This conjecture is raised into a certainty by the genealogy which follows, and with which the book closes."

The genealogy at the conclusion of the book is a

valuable contribution to the biblical narrative. In many respects, it is the most important document in the Old Testament. This we shall consider. "Now these are the generations of Pharez: Pharez begat Hezron, And Hezron begat Ram, and Ram begat Amminadab, And Amminadab begat Nahshon, and Nahshon begat Salmon, And Salmon begat Boaz, and Boaz begat Obed, And Obed begat Jesse, and Jesse begat David" (Ruth 4:18-22).

There are several observations that need to be made concerning this document. It is only a partial genealogy. It begins with Pharez and ends with David. Pharez was the son of Judah, according to the story in Genesis thirty-eight. This genealogy gives the vital link between Judah and David. The fact that the genealogy stops with David suggests that the Book of Ruth was written during the reign of David. Evidently it was not written beforehand.

One commentator calls attention to the fact that there are but fourteen generations given in the Bible. Eleven are listed in the Book of Genesis. The generations of Aaron and Moses are recorded in Numbers three. The last one given in the Old Testament is this account in Ruth. The fourth is found in Matthew one. Between David and Christ there is no genealogy given in the Old Testament. In the books of Ezra and Nehemiah are contained several genealogical tables, but they are those of the priests and others. David's line, the kingly seed, is not given, but the record of the kings who followed David up to the captivity is given in detail in the historical accounts of the kings.

There are two genealogical tables given in the

Gospels of Jesus Christ. They differ only in the fact that the record in Matthew starts with Abraham and follows the line down through Solomon, the son of David. This is evidently Joseph's line, and it gave to the Lord Jesus Christ the legal title to the throne of David. The record in Luke is given in reverse order from all other genealogies in the Bible. This should arrest the attention of the student of Scripture. There is a different genealogy given in Luke. It traces the line through Nathan, the son of David (Luke 3:31). Mary was evidently in the line that led through Nathan, and it is her genealogy which is given in Luke. From Mary, Christ received the bloodline that led through David. These facts are highly significant when considered in the light of a prophecy made concerning Jeconiah, king of Judah, who was in the line that led to Joseph. "As I live, saith the Lord, though Coniah the son of Jehoiakim king of Judah were the signet upon my right hand, yet would I pluck thee thence ... Thus saith the Lord, Write ye this man childless, a man that shall not prosper in his days: for no man of his seed shall prosper, sitting upon the throne of David, and ruling any more in Judah" (Jeremiah 22:24,30).

Compare this prophecy with Matthew 1:11 and a real difficulty will present itself. It would have been impossible for Christ to have been a natural son of Joseph and at the same time be the one chosen of God to sit upon the throne of David. There was a curse pronounced upon the legal line. Christ came from a prince of the house of David through his mother, Mary.

The genealogical table in Ruth is brought over into both of the tables in the Gospels. The table in Ruth is essential to both Matthew's and Luke's tables. In Luke's account, it is found in verses thirty-two and thirty-three of chapter three. Matthew's Gospel, which opens the New Testament, likewise begins with the genealogy. The New Testament rests upon the accuracy of that genealogy. The table from Ruth is included in the first chapter of Matthew from verse three to six. This genealogy from Ruth is the most vital link in the chain from Abraham to Christ. The table in Matthew is a duplication of the one in Ruth from Pharez to David, with a few details added to the one in Matthew. Four names are added, and they are not the names of men that apparently are left out of the table in Ruth. (There is an omission of some names from the pedigree in Ruth as has been pointed out by Kiel and Delitzch: ". . . some of the intermediate links must have been left out even here. But the omission of unimportant members becomes still more apparent in the statement which follows, *viz.*, that Nahshon begat Salmon, and Salmon Boaz, in which only two generations are given for a space of more than 250 years, which intervened between the death of Moses and the time of Gideon." The writer of Ruth was deliberately giving ten generations; therefore, the omissions are explained. Matthew's Gospel does not attempt to fill in these gaps.) These names are those of women and that seems altogether strange because women were omitted according to the commonly accepted practice of that day. Women did not count in a genealogy. Yet, we find four women mentioned

22

in Matthew. That is not the only exceptional feature about them. They are not only women but _Gentile_ women. Why are they included in Matthew's genealogy? Several writers have called attention to this unusual fact concerning the genealogy of Christ, and they have drawn beautiful lessons from it. Dr. Gaebelein has called particular attention to these four women. Kiel and Delitzsch earlier had drawn attention to three of these women: "As Judah begat Pharez from Tamar the Canaanitish woman (Genesis 38), and as Rahab was adopted into the congregation of Israel (Joshua 6:25), and according to ancient tradition was married to Salmon (Matthew 1:5), so the Moabitess Ruth was taken by Boaz as his wife, and incorporated in the family of Judah, from which Christ was to spring according to the flesh (see Matthew 1:3,5, where these three women are distinctly mentioned by name in the genealogy of Jesus)."

A consideration of these four women will enable us to acquaint ourselves with the pedigree in Ruth. Thamar is the first one mentioned in Matthew: "And Judas begat Phares and Zara of Thamar." The story of Judah and Tamar is told in Genesis thirty-eight, and it is a base story of fornication. Tamar was a Canaanitish woman who married Er, a son of Judah. Er was evil and the record says that God slew him. Onan, the next son of Judah, was apparently forced by his father to take Tamar, but he disobeyed, and the Lord likewise slew him. Judah told Tamar to wait until his youngest son was grown, and he would give him to her for a husband. Years passed and Judah did not keep his promise. So Tamar laid aside her widow's garments, and having clothed herself as a harlot, she went to Judah. Although he did not recognize her, he was committing a double sin. There were two sons born to Tamar, twins, Zarah and Pharez. Only the line of Pharez is followed in Scripture, as it is the chosen line. It is the genealogy of Pharez that we have in the Book of Ruth. The list opens with this statement: "These are the generations of Pharez."

In these four women's names, we have an outline of the plan of salvation. Tamar entered the genealogy of Christ although she was a sinner. God's plan of salvation rests upon the statement: "All have sinned, and come short of the glory of God" (Romans 3:23). Salvation rests upon the foundation that sin is a reality. A Saviour is for sinners. The Great Physician sought the sick, for well people do not need a doctor. The first step in obtaining salvation is for the sinner to come to God as a sinner.

"Just as I am, without one plea,
But that Thy blood was shed for me,
And that Thou bidd'st me come to Thee,
O Lamb of God, I come, I come."

God places all men on the same level. They are all listed at par value. All are sinners. He does this that he might save some. Otherwise, all would be lost.

The second name of a Gentile woman in the genealogy of Christ is Rahab, "And Salmon begat Boaz of Rahab." Rahab is usually identified in Scripture by her profession, "Rahab, the harlot." She lived in the city of Jericho, and when Joshua sent spies into the city, she received them. She believed in the God of Israel and believed that he was going to give the land to them. That was more than some of Israel believed. Rahab made this interesting confession to the spies: "And she said unto the men, I know that the Lord hath given you the land, and that your terror is fallen upon us, and that all the inhabitants of the land faint because of you. For we have heard how the Lord dried up the water of the Red sea for you" (Joshua 2:9,10). She heard and believed and God honored her faith, for he had not found so great faith in Israel. She obeyed the spies and placed the scarlet thread on the outside. Rahab was included in the genealogy of Christ because of her faith; and she is given a niche in the memorial gallery of faith. "By faith the harlot Rahab perished not with them that believed not, when she had received the spies with peace" (Hebrews 11:31).

Man has nothing to present to God in respect to works except the fruit of a cursed ground. The works of a sinner are not acceptable to God, yet God must require good works of man. The good works are faith. "Jesus answered and said unto them, This is the work of God, that ye believe on him whom he hath sent" (John 6:29). The only thing that a lost sinner can offer God is the feeble hand of faith. Faith is the means that God places in reach of man that he might avail himself of it in order to obtain salvation. "For by grace are ye saved through faith; and that not of yourselves: it is the gift of God" (Ephesians 2:8).

The third name of a Gentile woman in the gene-

alogy of Christ is Ruth. Although her name is omitted in the genealogy at the end, her story is told in
the book and that is evidently the reason why
Matthew included her name. The other two women
were great sinners but that is not true of Ruth.
Among the others, she is like a flower among weeds.
She possessed a fine character and there is not one
flaw found in her story; but the law kept her out of
Israel. A Moabite was forbidden to enter the
congregation of the Lord (Deuteronomy 23:3). She
had to have a redeemer who would put over her his
cloak of righteousness and right to the blessings of
God. He had to extend grace to her. This Boaz did,
as we have mentioned and will deal with fully
when we come to the story proper. Attention must
be called here to grace as the way by which she
entered the genealogy of Christ.

When a sinner reaches forth the feeble and
empty hand of faith to God, then God takes it with
the hand of grace that he has outstretched to a lost
world. "By grace are ye saved" is the testimony of
every sinner. The law condemns every sinner and
drives him from the presence of the Lord, like Cain.
"Therefore by the deeds of the law there shall no
flesh be justified in his sight: for by the law is the
knowledge of sin" (Romans 3:20). The law not only
excommunicated the sinner, but was unable to redeem him. Law, like the anonymous kinsman, cannot redeem without imperiling its own inheritance.
Law cannot lower its standard to man's level and
still be law. But a greater than Boaz has come and
he not only endangered his inheritance, but gave
his own life a ransom for many. Now the vilest

26

sinner can be saved by grace, "Being justified freely by his grace through the redemption that is in Christ Jesus" (Romans 3:24).

The fourth woman who is mentioned in the genealogy of Christ does not have her name given. "And David the king begat Solomon of her that had been the wife of Urias" (Matthew 1:6). Although her name is not given, her identity is not difficult to ascertain. She was Bathsheba, the wife of Uriah, the Hittite. Her name is concealed by the Holy Spirit, for the sin was David's and not hers. David committed adultery with her, and then to cover his sinful act, he deliberately had Uriah murdered. This is the one black spot on the life of David.

David was God's man and the man of whom God had said, "The Lord hath sought him a man after his own heart" (I Samuel 13:14). This was before David committed this crime, but God never took his hand off David. After committing the crime, David apparently thought he had escaped detection. It was the custom for kings to commit horrible crimes, and for no one to call them to account. But this was not true of God's king, for he could not act like those round about him. God sent Nathan, the prophet, unto David, and he pointed his finger at David before the interview was over and said, "Thou art the man." David repented of his sin when he could have had Nathan killed for accusing the king. David did not want anything to separate his soul and God. He had cried, "As the hart panteth after the water brooks, so panteth my soul after thee, O God" (Psalm 42:1). David was willing to pay for his sin, but he learned as he wrote, "Blessed is he whose transgression is forgiven, whose sin is covered" (Psalm 32:1). Trouble followed David all the remaining days of his life. This child of Bathsheba died; his own daughter was ruined; and his son Absalom led a cruel rebellion against him when David was an old man. Finally, Absalom was murdered, which broke old David's heart. He never whimpered under the hand of God nor complained, for David knew he had sinned and he wanted fellowship maintained between his soul and God.

After a sinner is saved by grace, he never reaches the plane of perfection in this life. He commits sins, but they do not destroy his salvation. They do destroy his fellowship, and these sins must be dealt with before fellowship can be restored. Another bore the penalty of these sins, and the Christian is commanded, "If we confess our sins, he is faithful and just to forgive us our sins, and to cleanse us from all unrighteousness" (I John 1:9). Confession is the way by which the prodigal son returns to the Father's house. A genuine Christian never reaches the exalted plane where he does not commit sin; and he does not reach the place where he will not confess it. David acknowledged his sin, but trouble, that will prompt the tenderhearted reader to ask God to withhold rather than increase, dogged his steps till his dying day. There is a law of God that is not abrogated even for the Christian: "Whatsoever a man soweth, that shall he also reap" (Galatians 6:7). This law is especially for Christians. God completely forgives the sinner and cleanses him from sin, but nevertheless this law operates in the physical world in which we live. A man may live a life of sin and wreck his body with drink, but confession of the sin will not remove the marks of transgression from the body. He will reap a harvest of pain and a wrecked body just the same.

There is an example of this in the New Testament. Saul stood and gave his consent to the stoning of Stephen. After Saul's conversion, he was taken outside of the city of Lystra on his first missionary journey and was stoned and left for dead. Apparently, Paul was dead, but God raised him up from the dead. That may have been the occasion when he was caught up into the third heaven. He learned that there must always be a harvest after seed-sowing in this world.

This chapter may well be concluded with a diagram of another on this genealogy that concludes the Book of Ruth. This is the genealogy of Pharez.

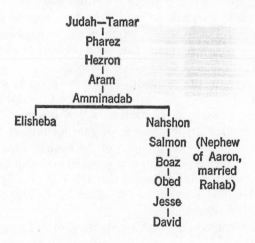

```
              Judah—Tamar
                   |
                 Pharez
                   |
                 Hezron
                   |
                  Aram
                   |
              Amminadab
         _____|_____
        |                         |
    Elisheba                  Nahshon
                                  |
                               Salmon   (Nephew
                                  |      of Aaron,
                                Boaz      married
                                  |        Rahab)
                                Obed
                                  |
                                Jesse
                                  |
                                David
```

CHAPTER 5

What Price Redemption

If the foregoing purposes for the Book of Ruth are not adequate to justify its inclusion in the Scripture, there would still be ample justification in the doctrinal purpose. This book presents in pictorial form one of the greatest doctrines of the Bible. One phase of the doctrine of redemption is presented in this book and nowhere else in Scripture. Redemption by a "kinsman-redeemer" is essential to a complete understanding of the doctrine of redemption. The contribution of the Book of Ruth to the subject of redemption is essential and all-important when it is considered that the Bible has been defined by Erdman as "the Book of Redemption unto the kingdom."

Redemption is possible only through a "kinsman-redeemer." God could not redeem apart from a mediator. Since only God could redeem, it became necessary for him to become that person. Under the subject, "Redemption for lost man to be sought in Christ," Calvin recognizes that God cannot redeem unless he "appears as a redeemer in the person of his only begotten Son." Again he affirms, "I only assert, that the happiness of the Church has always been founded on the person of Christ." Dr. Strong, in contemplating Christology, makes it synonymous with "The redemption wrought by Christ."

Not only is man confined to salvation by grace, which is the real "offense of the cross," but also God is confined to a redemption wrought by himself and made available to man only through the avenue of grace. Two alternatives confronted God. Either he could let man bear the penalty of his own sin and be eternally lost, or he could redeem man by himself paying the penalty. Apparently, there was no middle ground on which he could stand. The "kinsman-redeemer" is the only figure in the Bible that gives an adequate understanding of God as the redeemer.

It is true that Moses as the deliverer of the nation of Israel from Egypt furnishes a figure of Christ as the great deliverer from sin; but he in no way adumbrates Christ as the "kinsman-redeemer." The writer to the Hebrews makes the distinction between Moses and Christ: "Moses verily was faithful in all his house, as a servant," but "Christ as a son over his own house." It was God who was the Redeemer of Israel out of Egypt, and Moses was functioning in the capacity of a servant. A servant could never be a full figure of our great Redeemer.

Christ was the Son of God, acting in that capacity; therefore, it is written, "God was in Christ, reconciling the world unto himself." Redemption requires a figure that gives us to understand why Christ became a man in order to redeem us. Moses in no way illustrates this. Moses shows that God used a man, but does not reveal that God *became* a man. Redemption cannot be properly comprehended until some figure is found to illustrate the person and work of Christ. The book of Ruth supplies one aspect to this doctrine that is found nowhere else.

Moses was not an adequate figure of a redeemer because he had neither the power nor price of redemption. Boaz was a kinsman-redeemer who had both the price and power to function as a kinsman-redeemer in the capacity to which he was called. Therefore, Boaz furnishes the only figure for the "kinsman-redeemer" aspect of redemption which is so essential for any proper theory of the atonement. The commercial theory of the atonement would have been delivered from the unsavory reputation of a cold business transaction if it had been presented with the proper perspective of the "kinsman-redeemer." It was, therefore, a serious omission on the part of Jonathan Edwards, Calvin, Robinson, Anderson, Strong, *et al.*, to ignore the Book of Ruth in a history of redemption. Paul was careful to guard the doctrine of redemption from becoming a heartless transaction of buying and selling when he wrote: "But when the fulness of the time was come, God sent forth his Son, made of a woman, made under the law, to redeem them that were under the law, that we might receive the adoption of sons" (Galatians 4:4,5).

Christ became our kinsman according to the flesh. He was included in our genealogy; he intruded into the history of man; he became one of us; he came close to us. Someone has framed it in this beautiful picture: "He came a little baby thing that made a woman cry." But he was not involved in our fall. He was free from our slavery. Boaz was a kinsman of Elimelech, but he was not involved in the bankruptcy of his estate. He was not a poverty-stricken relative who could offer nothing but helpless sympathy. He was well able to redeem the estate from all claims. So, Christ was able to redeem us. He became a man but not bankrupt humanity, for he "was in all points tempted like as we are, yet without sin." He became like us, but not one of us. He was not a poverty-stricken relative, but he was "holy, harmless, undefiled, separate from sinners, and made higher than the heavens."

Boaz not only redeemed the estate of Elimelech, but he performed another work that only a kinsman-redeemer could do. It was the duty of the next of kin to marry the wife of the dead that he might raise up seed to the dead. In other words, the kinsman-redeemer preserved the name of the dead and furnished an heir to the estate. Boaz married the foreigner from Moab, the widow of Mahlon, the son of Elimelech, and he raised up that line once more. Christ has not only freed us from the slavery of sin; but he has brought us into the place where we are able to receive "the adoption of sons." This is personal, intimate and vital. Little wonder that Paul could utter this paean of praise regarding the

33

redemptive work of Christ: "I am crucified with Christ: nevertheless I live; yet not I, but Christ liveth in me: and the life which I now live in the flesh I live by the faith of the Son of God, who loved me, and gave himself for me" (Galatians 2:20). This is not a cold business deal but a love affair. It tells about one who came where we were, and became one of us that he might redeem us.

Another reason why God had to become our kinsman in order to redeem us is found in the price that was paid for our redemption. Although Boaz was not compelled to redeem the estate of Elimelech and the maid from Moab, according to the Mosaic law, if he did choose to act in that capacity, he had to be a kinsman. The law did not force the kinsman to act, but it did say that he must be a kinsman before he could act. He never could have been the redeemer and not be a kinsman. God could never have redeemed man, and we say this reverently, had he not become our kinsman. If he had been unwilling to leave heaven, then man would have had to go to hell. God did not have to redeem us, but if he did involve himself in that work, he had to become a man. The incarnation, therefore, begins quite properly the work of redemption. The virgin birth of Christ is essential to any satisfactory plan of salvation. He was made of a woman for purposes of redemption. Little wonder that Bethlehem became conspicuous in the Book of Ruth, for the Kinsman-Redeemer must be born there. The angelic salutation at his birth was not a meaningless statement: "For unto you is born this day in the city of David a Saviour, which is Christ the Lord"

34

(Luke 2:11). Love was the law that compelled Boaz to act. It was love that sent Christ from heaven to Bethlehem. "For God so loved the world, that he gave his only begotten Son."

Blood was the price of man's freedom from sin. It could not reasonably be the blood of bulls and goats. Human blood was required. It would have been the rankest sort of heathenism for any of the sons of Adam to have shed his blood for sin. It would have been valueless and vile. The sacrifice of human blood has been, and is, degrading for the natural man in sin. But God took upon himself flesh, and the blood of that body could be the only satisfactory price. It signified his kinship to us, but it also was not under the curse of sin.

"The precious blood of Christ" was the only legal tender that could redeem man. God paid this exorbitant price for the redemption of man because nothing less would do. The justice of God demanded the pound of flesh, and the pound of flesh was taken, but it required the bloodletting of Christ. Man had lost his life through sin, and his right to life. Man forfeited all claims to life when he disobeyed God in the garden. "Thou shalt surely die" is the inexorable law of God. Christ paid in the coin of life the penalty of man's sin. It was his blood. Therefore, "we have redemption through his blood, the forgiveness of sins, according to the riches of his grace" (Ephesians 1:7). The blood speaks not only of the heinousness of sin, but tells us that the one who made such a sacrifice was kin to us. The blood was the price of our redemption, but it was not a cold business deal. That blood came

35

from the warm heart of God, and it was made available for every man.

> "There is a fountain filled with blood,
>   Drawn from Immanuel's veins;
> And sinners, plunged beneath that flood,
>   Lose all their guilty stains."
> —*William Cowper*

CHAPTER 6

A Foolish Decision

"And not many days after the younger son gathered all together, and took his journey into a far country, and there wasted his substance with riotous living" (Luke 15:13). It is never a delightful story when a member of the chosen seed leaves the land of promise and goes into the far country. It makes no difference whether he is Abraham going into Egypt to escape the famine, or the prodigal son going to the far country and into the face of a famine there, the results are negative and the ending tragic. Elimelech should not have gone into the land of Moab, regardless of the conditions in the land of promise. Chapter one of the Book of Ruth tells the tragic story of a prodigal family, which has been duplicated many times in the course of human events, by individuals, by families and by nations.

The tragic story of Elimelech is to engage our attention in this chapter.

During the deep declension of the period of the judges, God instituted judgment after judgment as a warning to bring the people back to himself. The times of the judges were black enough, but these seasons of judgment were especially black. Famine was the stick of his correction and his customary method of judgment. Several times in the history of his people, he called for a famine as a means of judgment. Some of the most notable passages are these: II Kings 8:1; Jeremiah 16:3-13; Ezekiel 5:11-17. This famine enables us to form some opinion as to the approximate time during which the incidents recorded in the Book of Ruth occurred. Robert Lee suggests that this famine is referred to in Judges 6:3,4. If that inference is correct, and there is no reasonable objection to it, the incidents recorded in the Book of Ruth occurred during the time of Gideon. This harmonizes with the viewpoint of Kiel and Delitzsch: "The incidents described in the book fall within the times of the judges (chapter 1:1), and most probably in the time of Gideon." Gideon was the sixth judge and personally was one of the more outstanding ones, but the condition of the people nullified much that he had done. It is stimulating to think that in all likelihood, Gideon and Boaz were acquaintances. If that is true, then there would have been a mutual admiration for each other. Regardless of the time during the period of the judges that we attempt to identify the happenings of Ruth, the hour was a dark one, made doubly so by the presence of a famine, the telltale mark of flagrant sin and the displeasure of God.

In the first few verses of the first chapter of Ruth we have the story of another prodigal son. He left the father's house of bread and went into the far country of Moab. All this was in disobedience to the will of the father. This man lived as a member of the tribe of Judah in Bethlehem-judah. Bethlehem-judah means "house of bread and praise." How suggestive this is of the wonderful house of the Father! It speaks of plenty and peace. There probably was no famine in the land of Moab, for this was a judgment restricted to the chosen people. Their privilege, as the chosen people, increased the measure of their responsibility. God was judging them but not Moab. Moab was not called to the high place afforded Israel. However, God could have provided for his own in the place of blessing, and he would have made ample provision if they had but trusted him. Howbeit, the famine struck terror in their hearts but did not inspire trust of the heart. They migrated immediately to the land of Moab.

There is trouble always for the prodigal son in the far country. It is in the far country that he receives his whipping and not when he returns in repentance and confession to his natal hearth. The hickory stick is applied in the far country; new shoes and a robe await his return home. He gets kicks in the far country; he is showered with kisses at home. Tears of sorrow are shed in Moab, but tears of joy fall at Bethlehem.

Elimelech and his family are but one example of many prodigal sons in the Bible. Abraham was called out of Ur of the Chaldees and instructed to dwell in the land of Canaan. In his day there was a famine, the first of thirteen famines mentioned in the Bible. "And there was a famine in the land: and Abram went down into Egypt to sojourn there" (Genesis 12:10). Now, God had given no instructions to Abraham to leave the land of promise, but the constant trek of multitudes before his tent door, migrating to the land of Egypt, was too much for Abraham. He silently folded his tent and joined the parade. It was in the land of Egypt that Abraham acquired potentially all his future trouble. He became wealthy and procured an Egyptian maid. These contributed to his undoing. While he abode in Egypt, God did not appear to him; and this is all the more striking in view of the fact that when he returned, God immediately communicated with him.

Elimelech, for this was the man's name in the Book of Ruth, took his wife and two sons and followed the example of his father, Abraham, and left the land of Israel in the time of a severe famine. This was contrary to the will of God, and trouble was the inevitable outcome. Elimelech emigrated to the land of Moab. It is significant that the record contains this statement: "And they came into the country of Moab, and continued there" (verse two). It was bad enough to leave the town of Bethlehem, the place of bread, and a place which was to have future significance, but to go to the land of Moab made it doubly bad. To seek temporary relief in the land of Moab was doubly bad, but to take up residence there was a tragedy.

It is sometimes asserted that the prodigal son will

not stay in the far country, and that the pigsty is only a momentary experience. Here is the sad story of a prodigal son who stayed in the far country. He seemed to enjoy the swill of the sty more than the house of bread. The house of bread is better in a famine than the land of Moab in time of plenty. Elimelech and his two sons died in the land of Moab. When someone inquired concerning the fate of the prodigal son had he died in the pigsty, Dr. Harry Rimmer is reported to have answered in this splendid way: "Well, he would be a dead son and not a dead pig." The prodigal son, Elimelech, did die in the pigpen; but certainly we are bold enough to add that he was an Israelite out of the will of God, but nonethless one of the children of the covenant.

The family of Elimelech seems to have settled at first rather comfortably in the land of Moab. The two sons married daughters of Moab, which was contrary to the Mosaic law. "Neither shalt thou make marriages with them [Hittites, Girgashites, Amorites, Canaanites, Perizzites, Hivites and Jebusites]; thy daughters thou shalt not give unto his son, nor his daughter shalt thou take unto thy son" (Deuteronomy 7:3). One commentator takes the position that this passage only refers to the Canaanites but not to other Gentiles. This is too narrow a restriction of the law, and certainly in practice, the nation of Israel applied this law to all Gentiles. At the time of the return from the Babylonian captivity, this law included the Moabites specifically (Ezra 9:2). Nehemiah called attention to those who had made illegal marriages in his day. "In those days also saw I Jews that had married wives of Ashdod, of Ammon, and of Moab" (Nehemiah 13:23). Nehemiah used very extreme measures with them: "And I contended with them, and cursed them, and smote certain of them, and plucked off their hair, and made them swear by God, saying, Ye shall not give your daughters unto their sons, nor take their daughters unto your sons, or for yourselves" (Nehemiah 13:25).

Let it be said for the justification of Elimelech, the marriages were made after his death, according to the record. There, however, was apparently no objection raised by Naomi, the widow of Elimelech, to the marriage of her sons with Moabitesses. Jewish writers from early times have contended that the early deaths of Naomi's sons were divine judgments because of their unlawful relationships. The story before us concerns primarily one of these wives from Moab. She is Ruth, the Moabitess, who married Mahlon.

The meaning of the names in Scripture contributes oftentimes to a proper understanding of the passage in which they occur. This is definitely true in the Book of Ruth, and it will be profitable at this juncture to examine the names that occur in the first chapter of our story. Names in Bible times were not given to distinguish a person from Tom, Dick and Harry. A name was not only given to a person to identify that person among others but to suggest something regarding the character of the individual. (e.g., Jacob's name was changed to Israel because the one who had been a "supplanter" became a "prince with God." Christ changed the name of Simon to Peter, for Peter means "rock" and this quality was to characterize him henceforth.)

Ruth means "beauty" and "appearance," according to Gesenius. The root word means "to feed a flock." Brown, Driver and Briggs give "friendship" as a meaning of Ruth. All these meanings are suggestive. Ruth was beautiful, as we shall have occasion to mention subsequently. A pastoral picture of loveliness is suggested by the root word. The meaning that follows more closely the theme of the story is that of friendship. The friendship she extended to her mother-in-law has become proverbial as an expression of that which is best. She came as a stranger and foreigner into the land of Israel; but she found one there in the person of Boaz who was more than a friend. She was a stranger to the God of Israel, but she came to know him and to trust him. This friendship he honored in a most singular way, as we shall see.

Elimelech means "the God of the king." This man bore a royal name, but he apparently did not measure up to its intention. Naomi means "pleasant." This woman found life bitter in the land of Moab; but when she returned to the land of Israel, the fragrance of the meaning of her name appeared again in her life.

The two sons of Elimelech and Naomi are virtually unknown. Nothing is said concerning them, but their names convey a wealth of suggestion. The meaning of the names must have applied to their lives. Mahlon means "sick" and Chilion means "pining." Certainly neither one of them could have been a robust picture of health. Their untimely demise confirms the meaning of their names. The death of the two sons left two widows in the family. Now there were three widows.

There is another name here which needs to be considered. It is the name of the country to which this Jewish family fled in time of famine. Moab was the terminus of their trek from Bethlehem, and it was a name that was ominous in the ears of the children of Israel. There was a distant blood-relationship between Israel and Moab. Moab occurs first in connection with the flight of Lot from the city of Sodom. "And the firstborn bare a son, and called his name Moab: the same is the father of the Moabites unto this day" (Genesis 19:37). This verse completes the story that is one of the most sordid on the pages of Scripture. It reveals the depths of iniquity. Moab was the son of Lot by an incestuous union with his eldest daughter. Lot was the nephew of Abraham. The Moabite people, who constituted the country of Moab, sprang from this offspring of Lot. No mention is made on the pages of Scripture of the growth of the son of Lot to the nation of Moab, for Scripture is concerned with that nation only as it touches the chosen nation of Israel. The next reference to Moab occurs in the song of redemption in Exodus after the children of Israel crossed the Red Sea. In Exodus 15:15 mention is made of the mighty men of Moab. In the interval during which Israel was becoming a strong nation in the brickyards of Egypt, Moab was likewise becoming a strong nation. Moab occupied a place to the southeast of the Promised Land. They stood on the route of Israel from Egypt, blocking the way. Moab became a thorn in the side of Israel after they turned back at Kadesh-barnea. The wilderness experience of Israel is concerned to a great extent with Moab and the land of Moab. It appears that about this time the Amorites had subjugated the land of Moab. When the children of Israel overcame the Amorites in battle at Jahez, the victory struck terror into the hearts of the Moabites.

Balak, king of Moab, became frightened and sent for Balaam to come and curse Israel. His inability to conform to the desires of Balak is recorded in the Book of Numbers. It is not in our sphere to examine these different prophecies of Balaam; but there is one phrase in the fourth and last one that concerns Moab. "I shall see him, but not now: I shall behold him, but not nigh: there shall come a Star out of Jacob, and a Sceptre shall rise out of Israel, and shall smite the corners of Moab, and destroy all the children of Sheth" (Numbers 24:17). This is probably the prophecy that the magi had in their possession which helped bring them to Jerusalem in their search for the King of the Jews.

This strange prophecy contains some unique statements which might bear inspection; but we wish to call attention to the one where it is indicated that there would be enmity and strife between Israel and Moab. The "Star out of Jacob" will smite the country of Moab. It is not the fulfillment of this prophecy but the revelation of enmity between these two that concerns us. Balaam was not able to curse Israel; but he did accomplish a far more subtle thing, for he taught Balak to cast a

45

stumbling block before Israel. Israel began to mix with the Moabites; the people indulged in the most grievous sins and worshiped the idols of the Moabites. In spite of all this, Moab did not exhibit a friendly spirit toward Israel. This formed the basis for their exclusion from the nation: "Because they met you not with bread and with water in the way, when ye came forth out of Egypt; and because they hired against thee Balaam the son of Beor of Pethor of Mesopotamia, to curse thee" (Deuteronomy 23:4).

The unfriendly conduct of Moab was not forgotten by Israel during the period of the judges, which is contemporaneous with the story of Ruth. Jephthah sent the following message in his day to the king of Ammon: "Then Israel sent messengers unto the king of Edom, saying, Let me, I pray thee, pass through thy land: but the king of Edom would not hearken thereto. And in like manner they sent unto the king of Moab: but he would not consent: and Israel abode in Kadesh" (Judges 11:17).

In spite of the enmity that existed between Israel and Moab, God forbade Israel to fight with Moab for possession of their land. "And the Lord said unto me, Distress not the Moabites, neither contend with them in battle: for I will not give thee of their land for a possession; because I have given Ar unto the children of Lot for a possession" (Deuteronomy 2:9).

The land of Moab also had, however, an attraction for Israel, because there Moses died and the Lord buried him. Moses, in some respects, was a prodigal son on the way to the Promised Land; but he died on the route and was buried in the far country. Elimelech, Mahlon and Chilion were not the first Israelites who died and were buried in the far country.

The Moabites became the natural enemies of the children of Israel after they entered the Land of Promise. During the times of the judges, immediately preceding the events of our story, Moab had enslaved the children of Israel (Judges 3:12-14).

David subjugated the land of Moab during his reign (II Samuel 8:2-12). David uttered a very strange statement concerning Moab, but revealing nonetheless: "Moab is my washpot" (Psalm 60:8). The prophets denounced Moab as the enemy of God (Isaiah 15). The famous Moabite Stone contains a record of the bitterness that existed between Israel and Moab.

Nebuchadnezzar captured the Moabites; and they disappeared from history as a nation, but not as a race. During the time of the return under Nehemiah, the Moabites were identified as a race, but the nation had ceased to exist. Even at this late date, the Moabite retained his proverbial position as an enemy of Israel.

It seems strange that Elimelech would have gone to Moab in the first place, considering that Moab was not a name to conjure with, to the Jews. Stranger than this is the story of Ruth who came into the congregation of Israel and entered into the plan of God in a very intimate way. She is called Ruth, the Moabitess. She was a member of that hated and hating race. Little wonder that the Chaldee Targum puts it in this plain language: "And

47

they transgressed the edict of the word of the Lord, and took to themselves alien wives of the daughters of Moab."

Naomi, after the death of her husband and two sons, was no longer content to abide in the land of Moab. Reports emanating from the land of promise brought assurance that the famine had ended, and that there was bread in abundance in the house of bread. She had had enough of tragedy in the land of Moab; so she determined to set out for home and Bethlehem. Apparently both of her daughters-in-law were of the same mind and fully intended to make the return trip with her. Both would have continued in the journey with her, had not Naomi asked them to return to their own homes. She pronounced a blessing on each and commended both for their kindly treatment in dealing with their husbands, her sons, and also with her. The affection of Ruth and Orpah for their mother-in-law abolishes the common opinion and shopworn bromide regarding mothers-in-law. Here is a mother whose sons' wives evidently pleased her immensely. Also here are two women of Moab who do not bear the marks of their race.

The parting of these three is a typically feminine scene, marked by much weeping. There was much waving of damp handkerchiefs, and passionate embraces made the scene exceedingly touching. Ruth and Orpah were loathe to leave, and finally avowed that they would continue with Naomi. "We will return with thee unto thy people" (Ruth 1:10). Then, Naomi gave them a sensible talk from the woman's viewpoint (verses 11-13). The two young women needed a home and a husband. These could not be readily procured if they followed her, and anyway she did not want them to come on some false hope. She had no more sons and she had no notion of taking another husband. This bit of information prepared the way for some near kinsman to become the kinsman-redeemer for Ruth. If Naomi had been blessed with another son, it would have been incumbent upon him, under the Sinaitic code, to have married one of the daughters-in-law. "If brethren dwell together, and one of them die, and have no child, the wife of the dead shall not marry without unto a stranger: her husband's brother shall go in unto her, and take her to him to wife, and perform the duty of an husband's brother unto her" (Deuteronomy 25:5).

In view of the fact that Naomi had no other son, then the legal obligation fell on some relative outside of the immediate family. This information coming from Naomi is but preparation for Boaz to act as the kinsman-redeemer. This was good advice from an elder woman to younger women. She revealed to them how preposterous it would be for them to follow her, and at the same time, expect to have a home and children. This bit of advice for the young women occasioned more weeping, and the thought of parting forever produced a fresh flood of tears. This scene depicts the real affection of love that bound these three women together. It is noticeable and worthy of favorable comment.

This crisis brought out the real character of these two young women, and revealed the underlying difference between Ruth and Orpah. The record

49

brings it out in this striking manner. "And Orpah kissed her mother-in-law; but Ruth clave unto her" (verse 14). Orpah was emotional and ready to shower kisses upon Naomi; but the advice of Naomi had chilled her desire to follow, and she demonstrated her love through feelings. It was not so with Ruth. Ruth possessed real faith and love. She exhibited the stamina of one who not only ran well, but who was not hindered in obeying the truth. Ruth did not fall from grace in the climactic event of her career. She was willing to undergo the consequences of following Naomi, whatever they might be. This expression of faith on the part of Ruth was to be acknowledged of God and rewarded by him a hundredfold.

Ruth and Orpah demonstrate the two kinds of members in the Church—the professors and the possessors. Orpah made only a profession of faith, and there was failure at the climactic moment; Ruth possessed genuine faith, and it produced fruit and works. Paul says, "All men have not faith" (II Thessalonians 3:2). Orpah was in that class. As the remainder of the story demonstrates, Ruth possessed a faith that could only come from God. "By grace are ye saved through faith; and that not of yourselves: it is the gift of God" (Ephesians 2:8).

Naomi, realizing the firm decision of Ruth to accompany her, made a final but futile attempt to persuade Ruth to return to her own people and to her own religion, "unto her gods" (Ruth 1:15). Oddly enough, one of the inducements held out by Naomi to Ruth was the heathen idolatry of Moab. It seems strange that Naomi should have insisted upon this. One explanation in support of her conduct is that she was testing the mettle of the faith of Ruth. If it were genuine, she could not be driven back to idolatry. If it were not, there was no reason for her to continue with Naomi.

The very mention of the gods of the Moabites reveals that these young Moabite women were called upon to make a decision regarding their religion. A return to Moab meant a return to idolatry. They had evidently become worshipers of the God of Israel. Their departure from Naomi meant, for all practical purposes, the sacrifice of their new-found faith. There was a deeper reason than human affection; there was the heart's relation to the true God. This was a momentous decision in the lives of these young widows. This was the crucial test and the line of demarcation which was to separate them for eternity. This was the turning point in the lives of these two. They chose that day whom they would serve.

Orpah went back to idolatry. Nothing more is said of her. No word of commendation nor condemnation is spoken. Like Judas, she went to her place. The very silence of Scripture is sufficiently adequate and eloquent to tell of a life of tragedy. When Ruth chose to follow Naomi, she made a momentous decision for Jehovah and the true worship of him. Ruth chose God, and he chose her in the greatest plan of the ages: namely, the bringing of Jesus Christ into the world. Ruth made a choice for God when she elected to go with Naomi. That was the crisis moment of her life. She never stood again at the crossroads of her life to make a deci-

sion for eternity. After that moment, she had only
to walk the ordinary path of his leading. Ruth chose
the God of Israel and took her place of trust under
his wings. Orpah went backward to darkness, pa-
ganism, superstition and gloom. Ruth went onward
to the light of glory, truth and the light of life.

> One ship sails east
> And another west,
> By the selfsame winds that blow;
> 'Tis the set of the sails,
> And not the gales,
> That tells them the way to go!

> "Like the winds of the sea
> Are the waves of Time,
> As we voyage along through life;
> 'Tis the set of the soul
> That determines the goal,
> And not the calm or the strife!"

Ruth's answer to the urging of Naomi could have
been given only by a character of the highest
caliber—one who had decided for God. If a monu-
ment had been reared to Ruth, this certainly would
have been its inscription, and it deserved to be
chiseled in marble: "And Ruth said, Intreat me not
to leave thee, or to return from following after thee:
for whither thou goest, I will go; and where thou
lodgest, I will lodge: thy people shall be my people,
and thy God my God: where thou diest, will I die,
and there will I be buried: the Lord do so to me,
and more also, if ought but death part thee and me"

(Ruth 1:16,17). Robert Lee says, "There is nothing in human literature more beautiful than Ruth's address to her mother-in-law—it is sublime."

It is not only a literary gem but it is the decision of a noble character at a dramatic moment, expressed in the language of pathos, passion and poetry. Ruth made seven statements which constituted a vow that she never broke. These seven statements reveal definite progress in the development of her decisions. First, she asked Naomi to desist in requesting her to leave her, for she was determined to follow her. This was not merely a halfhearted decision but extended into all the ramifications of life. In the second place, she was determined to go wherever Naomi went. In the third place, she intended to live with her mother-in-law in whatever place Naomi went. She would share the same privations under the same roof. She locked her life intimately into that of Naomi. In the fourth place, she was leaving her people for good; and she was choosing Naomi's people forever. Ruth was willing to break down the agelong barrier of enmity and hatred and become one of the people of Israel. That was a tremendous decision for a member of the nation of Moab. In the fifth place, she was making a decision for God. She was leaving the idolatry of Moab permanently and was putting her trust in Jehovah forever. This was the supreme decision for Ruth. This was the primary point and the highest affirmation of the seven statements that Ruth made. In the sixth place, this was a decision for life. It extended through to death. But even in death she did not want to be separated from Naomi, and this constituted the seventh affirmation. She would be buried with her. She confirmed all this with an oath. The last statement is in the form of an oath that occurs frequently in the historical books of First and Second Samuel (I Samuel 3:17).

Naomi was thoroughly convinced that Ruth intended to go with her, and she refrained from further attempts to persuade her to abide in Moab. These two widows began the weary journey back to Bethlehem. They must have made a sad spectacle as they trudged along the road. The prodigal daughter was returning home, and it must have been a sad experience in the life of Naomi. But alas! it was filled with mingled feelings. How good home must have looked after years of absence! Her return and plight moved the city of Bethlehem to compassion. They were dazed to see the prodigal daughter return in the rags of poverty, and their only comment was, "Is this Naomi?" But there is always "joy in heaven" over the return of the prodigal. Naomi had left Bethlehem with a husband and two sons, but she returned with only a Gentile girl. She was given one stranger for three loved ones. This was not nearly so tragic as it appeared on the surface and as subsequent events proved. At the birth of Obed, the women of Bethlehem said to Naomi, "Thy daughter in law, which loveth thee, which is better to thee than seven sons, hath born him."

Evidently Elimelech was well-fixed in material things when he left the city of Bethlehem. Ten years of abode in the land of Moab, with its accompanying misfortunes, had reduced the family fortune to nil. This radical change of fortune, which was very evident when Naomi returned, touched the heart of the little town of Bethlehem. Then Naomi related her sad story with a complaining note. She requested that they no longer call her Naomi, but *Mara,* which meant that she no longer wanted to be called "pleasant," but "bitter," because the latter name conformed more closely to her appearance.

Nevertheless, Naomi committed the grievous error of placing the blame for all her trouble upon God by charging, "The Almighty hath dealt very bitterly with me." This has been symptomatic of the Adamic nature from the very beginning. Even Adam inferred that the woman whom God had given him was responsible for the presence of sin. He thereby threw the blame back into the lap of God, suggesting that if God had not given her to him, the tragedy of the fall would have been averted. The children of Adam have been making that and similar charges against God ever since. It was not God who had dealt bitterly with Naomi; she was reaping the fruit of the sin of disobedience. Naomi was but gleaning in the fields of a far country, away from the presence of God. God was not responsible for her misfortune, but he was responsible for the voice that had wooed her back home. It was the grace of God that was responsible for the blessing that was to come to her now that she had listened to the voice and returned. Glorious things were in prospect for her, but she was blinded to all that at this time.

She described the sad experience through which

she had passed in these striking words, "I went out full, and the Lord hath brought me home again empty." Quite evidently, the contrast between her former economic condition and her poverty when she returned was great. It was a long way on the economic scale from "full" to "empty." She had run the gamut. A family of four prosperous Bethlehemites had emigrated to Moab. The three male members had died and after ten years of adversity, the mother of the family returned with this daughter of the hated nation of Moab. The prodigal son mentioned in Luke 15 had no more bitter experience. Job had passed through no more excruciating time of adversity. Fuller has described the plight of Naomi in this very picturesque style: "Of the two sexes, the woman is the weaker: of women, old women are feeblest; of old women, widows most woeful; of widows, those that are poor, their plight most pitiful; of poor widows, those who want children, their case most doleful; of widows that want children, those that once had them, and after lost them, their estate most desolate; of widows that have had children, those that are strangers in a foreign country, their condition most comfortless. Yet all these met together in Naomi, as in the center of sorrow, to make the measure of her misery pressed down, shaken together, running over. I conclude, therefore, many men have had affliction—none like Job; many women have had tribulation—none like Naomi."

Naomi's insistence for a name that would be more in keeping with her plight was not complied with by the writer of this book, for in the very next verse it is asserted, "So Naomi returned." There was a blessing awaiting her back in Bethlehem that would have made the name "Mara" as unsuitable for her as she now supposed "Naomi" to be. Pleasant things were in store for her henceforth, and bitter experiences belonged back in the land of Moab. As the time of her peregrination was over, she would settle down in contentment in the house of bread, even though straitened circumstances were to continue for a short period.

Naomi and Ruth returned at a most propitious time. It was the season of the barley harvest. Dr. Davis says that the barley harvest was in April and began with the celebration of the Feast of Firstfruits. The barley was the firstfruits of that land and day according to Exodus 9:31,32. It was also at the conclusion of the rainy season while the Jordan River was overflowing (Joshua 3:1). It was the springtime and the season of firstfruits. To the Church this season and the Feast of Firstfruits speak of the resurrection of Christ, for he is "the firstfruits" in resurrection. Certainly it is not without significance that the Gentile stranger was brought into the blessings of God at the season which speaks of the resurrection of Christ. It was the death and resurrection of Christ that brought the Gentiles into the place of blessing in the Church. "Wherefore remember, that ye being in time past Gentiles in the flesh, who are called Uncircumcision by that which is called the Circumcision in the flesh made by hands; that at that time ye were without Christ, being aliens from the commonwealth of Israel, and strangers from the cove-

57

nants of promise, having no hope, and without God in the world: but now in Christ Jesus ye who sometimes were far off are made nigh by the blood of Christ ... Now therefore ye are no more strangers and foreigners, but fellowcitizens with the saints, and of the household of God" (Ephesians 2:11-13,19). This typical interpretation is certainly not fanciful, as it coincides with the facts concerning the Church. The Gentiles came into blessings by the death and resurrection of Christ. It was springtime and the time of the Feast of Firstfruits when Ruth came to Bethlehem.

Too much stress cannot be placed upon the entrance of Ruth into Bethlehem. It was not only a beautiful picture of the Church, but it marked the moment which was to bring fame to Bethlehem. Likewise, God was going to take this event which was marked with simplicity and pathos, and he was going to crown it with glory and honor. In the eternal counsel of an omnipotent God, this forlorn Gentile girl, the insignificant village of Bethlehem and the apparently nonessential circumstances which brought them together were to be lifted out of the commonplace and made to shine with divine light. Thus was God moving in that out-of-the-way village in the far-off yonder time with a down-and-out individual.

CHAPTER 7

A Chance Meeting

". . . and the greatest of these is love" (I Corinthians 13:13, A.R.V.).

> "The fragrant sheaves of the wheat
> Made the air above them sweet;
> Sweeter and more divine
> Was the scent of the scattered grain,
> That the reaper's hand let fall
> To be gathered again
> By the hand of the gleaner:
> Sweetest, divinest of all,
> Was the humble deed of thine,
> And the meekness of thy demeanor."
> —*Longfellow*

We have introduced to us in chapter two the last principal character in this story. He is Boaz, a kinsman of Naomi, and the hero of our story. His name means "in whom is strength." Delitzsch rejects this meaning but gives "alacrity" as the correct meaning. Both meanings could readily apply to the character of the one who possessed this name in our story. He is called a "mighty man of wealth." The Chaldee gives the phrase "mighty in the law" as a third possible rendering for this expression which describes Boaz. It is the same phrase that occurs in the Book of Judges for the deliverers. This is the same expression that the angel used to address Gideon (Judges 6:12). Certainly, the expression as used with reference to Gideon did not connote wealth. There is a Jewish tradition that associates Ibzan, one of the judges (Judges 12:8), with Boaz. Ibzan was from Bethlehem and the tradition does have some support. From the foregoing, it is quite permissible to conjecture that Boaz was an outstanding man of his day, a man of character and strength. What a contrast he must have been to Mahlon, the first husband of Ruth, whose name and life speak of weakness and frailty! All three of the suggested meanings reveal an aspect of the character of this great soul. Each one presents some aspect of his life which the Spirit purposed to reveal.

On the canvas of God's Word, Boaz is drawn with noble features. He fulfilled in his life all that the Latin suggests in the great word *virtus*. Boaz was a man of virtue in the literal sense of that word. There is not a more winsome character presented in the Old Testament than that of Boaz; and

there is not a more lovely woman in the Bible than
Ruth. She compares favorably with her descendant
Mary, the mother of Jesus. These two, Ruth and
Boaz, stand out like stars on the black background
of that corrupt day. Boaz was a wealthy kinsman of
Naomi. The first verse uses a word that does not
convey that strong meaning; but a word used later,
which we will consider, does so. We shall reserve
for a succeeding chapter the consideration of Boaz
as the kinsman-redeemer. His position of wealth
made it possible for him to redeem the estate of
Elimelech. In the suggestion that Boaz was a man
of valor, there is found an explanation why he had
not met Ruth when the two widows first returned.
He was probably away at the time on some military
expedition which prevented him from meeting the
comely Moabitess. As a man who was mighty in the
law, he is revealed as one who was acquainted with
the Mosaic law. He possessed a knowledge of the
Word of God. The implications in the remainder of
the story support this interpretation of the text. He
revealed an easy familiarity with the technicalities
of the law.

Boaz as the kinsman-redeemer is a figure of the
Lord Jesus Christ, our Kinsman-Redeemer. There is
not a finer and truer type of the Lord Jesus Christ
in the Bible than Boaz. Ruth, as the Gentile redeemed by grace, is a glorious picture of the
Church as the bride of Christ to be presented to
him "without spot or blemish."

Ruth accepted her poverty in humbleness and
quietness, and she sought to make the best of an
unfortunate situation. She did not rebel against the

pinch of penury, but requested her mother-in-law for permission to go and glean in the fields. These two must have been in danger of starving. Her request revealed that she was acquainted with the Mosaic law. Otherwise, how would she have known that it was possible for her, a stranger, to glean in the fields? The Moabites possessed no such just law. God's wonderful arrangement for taking care of the poor among his people reveals his great concern for them. There was an expressed law, which was given that the poor might have adequate provisions made for their needs: "And when ye reap the harvest of your land, thou shalt not wholly reap the corners of thy field, neither shalt thou gather the gleanings of thy harvest" (Leviticus 19:9). "And when ye reap the harvest of your land, thou shalt not make clean riddance of the corners of thy field when thou reapest, neither shalt thou gather any gleaning of thy harvest: thou shalt leave them unto the poor, and to the stranger: I am the Lord your God" (Leviticus 23:22). "When thou cuttest down thine harvest in thy field, and hast forgot a sheaf in the field, thou shalt not go again to fetch it: it shall be for the stranger, for the fatherless, and for the widow: that the Lord thy God may bless thee in all the work of thine hands" (Deuteronomy 24:19).

Poverty is in no way a blessing. Contrariwise, it is a curse. It was part of the curse that Christ bore. It was no proud confession but a sad admission that he made to the scribe who sought to follow him, "The foxes have holes, and the birds of the air have nests; but the Son of man hath not where to lay his head" (Matthew 8:20). It is possible to become so involved in the Sabbath question raised by the Pharisees when his disciples were gathering corn on the Sabbath day that the raw fact of the hunger of his disciples is completely ignored. Following him meant hunger to them. "He became poor" in material things, for poverty is one of the results of sin. One of the most marvelous things prophesied concerning our Lord in the kingdom is: "But with righteousness shall he judge the poor" (Isaiah 11:4). The poor will some day enter a new era, and then poverty will be removed from this earth. Man's utopias cannot remove poverty; only the coming of the King can do that.

Riches in and of themselves constitute no evil. God is rich, and he makes that claim concerning himself: "For every beast of the forest is mine, and the cattle upon a thousand hills" (Psalm 50:10). One of the promises made concerning those who enter the Father's house is that they will inherit riches. I care not whether this be considered literally or spiritually; the children of the Father shall lack no good thing and shall inherit some day with Christ. Christ is wealthy beyond the dreams of Croesus. "He was rich ..." It is God's intention to abolish poverty in his universe by making wealthy all those who enjoy it. Under the theocracy of Israel, God made adequate provision for the poor.

Ruth was but exercising her prerogative under the theocracy of Israel. Strangers were permitted to go into the fields of those who were harvesting grain and gather what the reapers left in the field. Ruth qualified in a twofold way: she was a stranger and a widow. Many wealthy and miserly farmers disobeyed this law as they did all the other laws. Therefore, the poor probably had to search diligently sometime before they found a field in which they could glean. A farmer who permitted the poor to glean in his field was a keeper of the Mosaic law in this respect. It spoke well of any who did this.

Evidently, when Ruth went out of the city of Bethlehem into the surrounding fields to glean, she had no definite destination in mind. We are informed that she chanced to enter the field of Boaz. The Old English in the Authorized Version has it: "And her hap was to light on a part of the field belonging unto Boaz" (Ruth 2:3). Delitzsch and Kiel give this literal translation: "Her chance chanced to hit upon the field ... " For Ruth it was the barest kind of a coincidence. On the human side, it was the fortuitous concurrence of circumstances. At this time Ruth had not even so much as heard of Boaz. Not until she returned at the conclusion of that day did she learn from the lips of Naomi, "The man is near of kin unto us, one of our next kinsmen."

There are multitudes who would interpret the episode of that day as fate. In the program of God, there is no such thing as fate, chance or accident. As the remainder of the story well illustrates, this was not chance, but the leading of the unseen hand of God. All this happened according to his direction. This was one instance out of millions of the providential dealings of God in the everyday affairs of man. Cromwell said: "Let us look into providences; surely they mean somewhat. They hang so together; have been so constant, so clear, so unclouded." He was moving all events in the life of this foreigner that she might occupy a strategic position and be an important link in the scarlet chain running through Scripture.

In the final analysis, no accident can happen to a child of God. He may be in a car wreck or he may be killed instantly; but for the child of God that cannot be finally defined as an accident. Nothing can come to a Christian that does not first receive the permission of God. Chance is removed from the child of God, for he is like Job of whom Satan said, "Hast not thou made an hedge about him?" The Christian can arise amidst the alarming vicissitudes of life and affirm, "And we know that all things work together for good to them that love God, to them who are the called according to his purpose" (Romans 8:28).

Ruth found herself unwittingly in the field of Boaz, unaware of the great events which were presently to ensue in her life. Boaz had been absent from the harvest field, attending probably to some urgent business in Bethlehem which detained him in the early part of the morning. As he entered the harvest field, he addressed the laborers with a most unusual greeting, "The Lord be with you." Virtually every commentator calls special attention to the form of greeting. First of all, it reveals the close relationship which existed between Boaz and the reapers. There was no labor problem in his field. Capital and labor were on speaking terms, and these were of the friendliest sort. The most remarkable part is the inclusion of the Lord's name, and a gracious recognition of him in all relationships of life. To his "The Lord be with you," they responded with the cheery and gracious greeting, "The Lord bless thee." God was reverently recognized in the harvest field by both the owner and the laborers. This all transpired in the days of the judges when there was decline, decay and disintegration. The remainder of Israel might forget God and turn to idols, but there was one man who did not forget him, but remembered him even in the extension of a morning greeting.

Observing the presence of a stranger, and an attractive one, Boaz inquired of the servant, who was acting as an overseer of the reapers, concerning her identity. "Whose damsel is this?" betrays more than a passing interest on the part of Boaz. It was love at first sight. The fact that Boaz had fallen desperately in love with Ruth is not concealed in the Book of Ruth. The love of man and woman is an arrangement of God, and is never wrong except when perverted by sin.

There are those who see in Boaz an old man well past the meridian of life. This is based on an extreme but general interpretation of Ruth 3:10 where Boaz commended Ruth in this manner: "And he said, Blessed be thou of the Lord, my daughter: for thou hast shewed more kindness in the latter end than at the beginning, inasmuch as thou follow-edst not young men, whether poor or rich." There is no positive statement here that Boaz was an old man, nor does the passage imply that Boaz was making a contrast between the young men and himself, in respect to their ages. Ruth, as a young widow, had not attached herself to the young set of her day in order to make a marriage for herself. Boaz called attention to the fact that she had followed neither poor nor rich. Ruth was not attempting to get married, and, therefore, had not followed the younger men who were eager to get married. The normal inference from this passage is that Boaz was not a boy but a man of middle age. Quite evidently, he was in the full vigor of manhood and not a dyspeptic man, approaching senility. The tenor of the story contradicts any such notion. The meeting of Ruth and Boaz involved a man who could in no sense be an old man.

The servant of Boaz identified Ruth as "the Moabitish damsel that came back with Naomi out of the country of Moab." Then the overseer explained Ruth's presence in the field of Boaz. With that bit of information, Boaz addressed Ruth with more than common courtesy. He insisted that she abide in his field and avail herself of the provision and protection which he had established for his maidens who were workers in the harvest. In the time of the judges, it was very likely unsafe for a young woman to go unchaperoned into the harvest fields to enjoy the benefits granted by the Mosaic law to the poor and to strangers. Boaz realized that an attractive woman like Ruth would jeopardize her womanly position; and some unscrupulous person might take advantage of her because of her straitened circumstances. Boaz offered to place the mantle of his protection about her. Boaz urged her to go "go not to glean in another field."

Moorhouse calls attention to a beautiful comparison here with Christ and the Church. The field belonged to Boaz. The fields of Boaz stretched over the entire landscape. It was not necessary for Ruth to go into another field, for there was plenty in the field of Boaz. The fields of Boaz were ample to supply more than the needs of Ruth. Christ has said to his Church, "Love not the world, neither the things that are in the world" (I John 2:15). There is enough for the Christian in Christ; therefore it is not necessary for the Christian to glean in the fields of the world.

Ruth realized that Boaz had passed the bounds of ordinary courtesy, and she demonstrated an admirable humility in response to this gracious provision. "Then she fell on her face, and bowed herself to the ground, and said unto him, Why have I found grace in thine eyes, that thou shouldest take knowledge of me, seeing I am a stranger?" (Ruth 2:10). Ruth recognized that she was the recipient of grace, and she knew that she had done nothing to merit it. "Surely he scorneth the scorners: but he giveth grace unto the lowly" (Proverbs 3:34). In thankfulness she fell on her face, according to the Eastern custom; and as the text indicates, she bowed down to the ground. What thankful humility on her part was manifested by this act! As we have previously shown, Ruth was included in the genealogy of Christ because of the grace of Boaz extended to her in this time of need.

Although heretofore Boaz had not met the Moabitish maiden, he had heard much concerning her. It was a good report and revealed that Ruth, a stranger, had won her way into the hearts of the natives of Bethlehem simply by her noble character and sterling worth exemplified in her dealings with her mother-in-law. It was common knowledge in Bethlehem that Ruth was exceptionally good to her husband's mother; and this conduct had ingratiated her to the Bethlehemites. She had chosen to forsake the place of her nativity to make a home with her adopted mother. Likewise, it was known that she had made a decision in favor of the "Lord God of Israel, under whose wings thou art come to trust," against the idols of Moab. Ruth's decision was for God, and by it she had found grace. All of this favorable comment had come to the ears of Boaz. It is comforting to note, in this connection, that Christ knows our hearts and understands thoroughly those little things that we do for him, but which go unnoticed by an indifferent world.

Ruth accepted the gracious hospitality extended to her, and acknowledged that the act of Boaz had brought comfort to her heart. She recognized and called attention to the fact that she was a stranger and "not like unto one of thine handmaidens." Wittingly, or unwittingly, she called attention to the very fact that had directed the attention of Boaz to her. We might say, adopting the common colloquialism of the street, "Ruth was different." Her unlikeness to the other maidens drew from the heart of Boaz the interested inquiry, "Whose damsel is this?" These facts confirm the suggestion that the meaning of Ruth is "beauty." The physical beauty of the Gentile girl, together with her beautiful character, found a responsive chord in his heart.

There is a modern but false notion that beauty is something that God cannot use. This pseudo piety is encouraged by the prevailing custom of prostituting beauty on the altar of mammon. But beauty, like any other gift of God (*e.g.*, a good voice), can be dedicated to the service of God. Modern youth needs to be reminded of this. The very interesting and suggestive feature about this entire episode is the silence of the record as to the physical appearance of Ruth. The beauty of her character, however, assumes great prominence in the account.

Boaz continued to make ample provision for the comely stranger who had wandered into his field through the direct providence of God. At noontime, Boaz invited her to partake of the midday meal with him and his workers. This portion of the story bears all the earmarks of a very modern and up-to-date story. He met her sometime during the late morning and invited her to lunch with him the same day. The rapidity with which these events occurred compares favorably with the acceleration of the machine age. Perhaps this decadent age, in spite of its vaunted improvement, is not far removed from the similar period in the days of our story.

Boaz granted her full liberty to glean where she pleased in the afternoon. He went so far as to instruct his reapers to leave some grain in her path. "And let fall also some of the handfuls of purpose for her, and leave them, that she may glean them, and rebuke her not" (Ruth 2:16). Pastor James Smith drew from this verse the subject for his series of volumes entitled, "Handfuls of Purpose." Boaz, by this conduct, was showing marked attention to Ruth, which fact could not escape the observation of the workmen and maidens in the field. Ruth herself could not have been oblivious to his magnanimous gesture on her behalf. Due to this generous consideration, Ruth gleaned that day "about an ephah." This was about one bushel and three pints. She returned to Naomi with the fruit of her labor at the end of that first day.

Not only had Boaz made it possible for her to glean this great amount, but Ruth had been diligent in the task. She "continued even from the morning," all through the day, "until even." This is a virtue that commends itself to every Christian and receives the full sanction of Scripture. "Not slothful in business; fervent in spirit; serving the Lord." Ruth was a woman of faith, but she was likewise found faithful in every task. True faith produces faithfulness. "Faith without works is dead." Although Boaz extended to her extraordinary privileges, she did not fail to avail herself of them and to apply herself to the task all that day. She never would have filled her bushel basket if she had not labored. The sheaves may be filled with grain; but it requires work to fill a bushel container with the ripened grain.

We sometimes sing rather lustily, "We shall come rejoicing, bringing in the sheaves," and then we go out and do nothing. Two things are essential if we are to come bringing "precious seed." One is prayer, and the other is to go, ourselves, into the fields and glean. Christ gave these as the essential requirements. "Then saith he unto his disciples, The harvest truly is plenteous, but the labourers are few; pray ye therefore the Lord of the harvest, that he

71

will send forth labourers into his harvest" (Matthew 9:37,38).

In the first place, the disciples were to pray that laborers might be sent forth into the harvest. That did not terminate their task. In the very next chapter, Christ called his disciples to him, and he commanded them to "go rather to the lost sheep of the house of Israel" (Matthew 10:6). After his crucifixion and resurrection, he enlarged the commission to include the world. "Go ye into all the world, and preach the gospel to every creature" (Mark 16:15). The normal and logical order is "pray" and "go." The Christian who is not out in the harvest field somewhere, somehow is failing in the very first essential of Christian living. A living faith is a going faith; a vital faith is an evangelizing faith. Calvin's comment is apropos: "Faith alone saves, but the faith that saves is not alone." Every Christian ought to be in the field of the One who is greater than Boaz. If he goes into the field to glean, he will find that some "handfuls of purpose" have been left by Christ, which will enable him to do more than glean. He will reap a bountiful harvest in white fields.

The full basket of Ruth caused Naomi to ejaculate, "Blessed be he that did take knowledge of thee" (Ruth 2:19). This bountiful supply could not have been the fruits of gleaning. Ruth related the incidents of that day, which events furnished an explanation for the full grain sack. Naomi probably hoped that Boaz had fallen in love with Ruth; and her woman's heart suspected, in view of the circumstances, that her hopes were fulfilled. Naomi, in

72

turn, informed her concerning Boaz and his kinship to them. Naomi calls him "one of our next kinsmen." The word used here for kinsmen is the Hebrew word *goel*. This is not the same word used in the first verse of this chapter. Here it means all that the word "kinsman-redeemer" implies. It indicated that Boaz was in the position, by blood relationship, to redeem the estate of Elimelech and to fulfill the duty of a kinsman by marrying Ruth. All this was implied in the word that Naomi employed. The word *goel* indicated more than merely a relation, and our story demonstrates the truth of that. We shall reserve for a subsequent chapter a full discussion of the word *goel*.

Naomi confirmed the action of Boaz by encouraging Ruth to follow him in his suggestions. "And Naomi said unto Ruth her daughter-in-law, It is good, my daughter, that thou go out with his maidens, that they meet thee not in any other field" (Ruth 2:22).

The concluding verse of this second chapter shows that the first day's experience was only a precursor of many that followed. "So she kept fast by the maidens of Boaz to glean unto the end of barley harvest and of wheat harvest; and dwelt with her mother-in-law" (verse 23).

Ruth went daily into the field of Boaz until barley harvest was ended. It is natural to infer that the first meeting of Boaz with Ruth was not the last, and the record of this first day was but typical of many that followed. To recognize this is sufficient preparation for the incidents in the next chapters. It is not an interpolation of this verse to add that the love of Boaz was deepened by constant contact, and that their friendship blossomed into mutual admiration and adoration for each other. Ruth continued to hold Boaz in high regard and esteem; and he, in turn, respected her nobility of character, which was studded with many virtues.

We may be sure that by the end of barley harvest, Boaz, the rich kinsman, and Ruth, the stranger from Moab, were in love. The entire town of Bethlehem must have smiled when they saw that the town's most acceptable bachelor had fallen in love with a girl from Moab, whom they, too, had taken into their hearts. The beauty of this story, which occurred during the time of men like Gideon, of whom it is written "he had many wives," and Samson, whose affairs with the opposite sex were notorious, would touch the hardest heart with profound wonder of the love of a great man for a noble woman. The honest love of a great man and a good woman is born in the heart of God; and this kind of love is noble and ennobling, and is described in the poetry of the Holy Spirit: "for love is strong as death . . . Many waters cannot quench love, neither can the floods drown it: if a man would give all the substance of his house for love, it would utterly be contemned" (Song of Solomon 8:6,7).

CHAPTER 8

A Planned Meeting

"Whatever hypocrites austerely talk
    Of purity, and place, and innocence,
    Defaming as impure what God declares
Pure, and commands to some, leaves free to all,
    Our Maker bids increase."

—Milton

"Then Naomi her mother in law said unto her,
My daughter, shall I not seek rest for thee, that it
may be well with thee" (Ruth 3:1)? It is more likely
that the "rest" referred to in this verse is marriage.
This has been the generally accepted interpretation,
and it is a sound one. Ruth's marriage into the
family of Naomi had brought travail to her heart.
She had tasted the bitter fruits of disappointment
and felt the keen pangs of sorrow. She had come in

contact with the seamy side of life, and had learned of the relentless struggle for a livelihood that raw poverty brings. Life in the presence of penury could not have been pleasant for the maid from Moab, but there is not a scintilla of suggestion that she ever complained. She had cast her lot with Naomi on the side of God, and she abode with fortitude in her decision. The mother-heart of Naomi went out to her daughter-in-law, and she sought for her a place of rest. This could only be attained in the quiet shelter of a godly home, where some strong man protected her from the stormy winds of a harsh world. The injunction of Paul in this connection has always been the mind of God. "I will therefore that the younger women marry."

This suggests the heart-cry of Christ for those who know the sting of sin and have borne the burdens of life: "Come unto me, all ye that labour and are heavy laden, and I will give you rest" (Matthew 11:28). The soul of the sinner needs to find rest. There is no rest in the world, but "there remaineth therefore a rest to the people of God" (Hebrews 4:9). This rest is found only in Christ. If we have found rest for our souls in Christ, we should seek, like Naomi, rest for some other storm-tossed sinner.

Naomi suggested the possibility of marriage. This was the evident tenor of her question when she asked, "Shall I not seek rest for thee, that it may be well with thee?" She appointed herself in the role of matchmaker. This should not be a cause for criticism of Naomi, for she was engaged in a worthy cause that had the sanction of God. Naomi's proposal was discreet and in no way transgressed the bounds of propriety. She was accepting the role of mediator in marriage. She not only suggested marriage but named the one whom Ruth should marry.

This was not a groundless proposal, as the events of the barley harvest bore mute but eloquent witness. Boaz had made all proper overtures, and Naomi's suggestion to Ruth was to make it possible for Boaz to know of her willingness and to encourage further negotiations. According to the Mosaic system, it was incumbent upon Ruth to make a definite move, especially after the events of barley harvest had occurred. If Ruth had remained taciturn, after Boaz had shown his interest in her during the harvest season, it would have constituted a rejection of him as a suitor for her hand. This was made necessarily so, as we have heretofore indicated, by the very strange custom instituted by the Mosaic system.

Boaz was a *goel,* and as such, it was his duty to marry the widow of a kinsman, provided he was next of kin. It was the duty of the widow to claim this provision for her interest, if she so desired. It was a false modesty and a weakness that would keep her silent. She was fulfilling God's intention for her if she asserted her rights, as given in God's law. Here is the very strange law: "If brethren dwell together, and one of them die, and have no child, the wife of the dead shall not marry without unto a stranger: her husband's brother shall go in unto her, and take her to him to wife, and perform the duty of an husband's brother unto her. And if the man like not to take his brother's wife, then let his brother's wife go up to the gate unto the elders, and say, My husband's brother refuseth to raise up unto his brother a name in Israel, he will not perform the duty of my husband's brother. Then the elders of his city shall call him, and speak unto him: and if he stand to it, and say, I like not to take her; then shall his brother's wife come unto him in the presence of the elders, and loose his shoe from off his foot, and spit in his face, and shall answer and say, So shall it be done unto that man that will not build up his brother's house. And his name shall be called in Israel, The house of him that hath his shoe loosed" (Deuteronomy 25:5, 7-10). According to this law, Ruth was the one to take the initiative and prosecute her case. Her condition was not the same as that of an unmarried woman. In that case, the man was to take the initiative. As a widow, it was incumbent upon her to let her intention be known to the kinsman. If the kinsman refused her proposal, she could hale him into court and bring disgrace upon him. Only ignorance could lead one to maintain that the Mosaic law was in favor of the man and that a woman had no rights under it. Here is but one case out of many where a woman was protected by the law.

The evident interest of Boaz furnished Naomi with confidence and Ruth with assurance. His conduct opened up the way for Ruth to request with boldness that he act as kinsman-redeemer for her. Boaz went as far as he could, under the law, toward making a marriage with the Moabitess. Quite frankly, it was now her move. The step that Naomi proposed to Ruth must be examined, therefore, under the light of the Mosaic law, and under the events of the barley and wheat harvest that year. When so viewed, any thought of presumption on the part of Naomi, or immodesty or brazenness on the part of Ruth, must be dismissed as utterly ridiculous. Only a prudish mind can find anything improper in the incident of chapter three, after all the facts are considered fairly. Kitto says that there was "nothing in these directions which was considered improper under the special and peculiar circumstance of the case." "Wash thyself therefore, and anoint thee, and put thy raiment upon thee, and get thee down to the floor: but make not thyself known unto the man, until he shall have done eating and drinking. And it shall be, when he lieth down, that thou shalt mark the place where he shall lie, and thou shalt go in and uncover his feet, and lay thee down; and he will tell thee what thou shalt do" (Ruth 3:3,4).

Until the events in this chapter, Ruth was evidently attired in widow's weeds. She wore the badge of mourning out of respect for the dead. Time had elapsed sufficiently now for the wounds to be healed, and the heart was occupied with another. It was Naomi, the mother of the deceased husband of Ruth, who suggested that she substitute for her garments of mourning a raiment that was more in harmony with her bright beauty. For Ruth, this meant breaking the last thread that tied her to an unhappy past in the land of Moab. The garments of mourning were fit symbols of her past, but now the future loomed before her, blazing with light and joy. For Ruth, "old things are passed away; behold, all things are become new."

The barley harvest was over, and the time for threshing and winnowing had come. An understanding of the harvest season of that day furnishes a background on which the proceedings of this chapter were enacted. James A. Patch gives the following description of the threshing process in that day: "The threshing floors are constructed in the fields, preferably in an exposed position in order to get the full benefit of the winds. If there is a danger of marauders they are clustered together close to the village. The floor is a level, circular area twenty-five to forty feet in diameter, prepared by first picking out the stones, and then wetting the ground, tamping or rolling it, and finally sweeping it. A border of stones usually surrounds the floor to keep in the grain. The sheaves of grain which have been brought on the backs of men, donkeys, camels, or oxen, are heaped on this area, and the process of tramping out begins. In some localities several animals, commonly oxen or donkeys, are tied abreast and driven round and round the floor ... Until the wheat is transferred to bags some one sleeps by the pile on the threshing floor."

Boaz had joined his laborers in the work of threshing the grain. A multitude had gathered there, some even bringing their families. It was a time of celebrating with profuse expressions of joy, when man made vocal his gratitude to God for his gracious provision in a bountiful harvest and expressed his appreciation for God's abundance; it was a season with a definite religious meaning. Boaz, though a rich man, joined his workmen in this happy occasion. It is not pure speculation to suggest that on the threshing floor of Boaz the religious significance was kept in the foreground. It was truly a festival unto Jehovah.

They were winnowing the grain at night to get the advantage of the night wind of that country, which was ideal for that process. Winnowing consisted of picking up the grain with some instrument, after it had been tramped out, and then pitching it into the wind that the chaff might be blown away. After the workmen had labored into the night, and the wind had abated, they ate a midnight meal, and then retired for the night there on the threshing floor that they might stand guard over the winnowed grain.

Naomi instructed Ruth how to proceed, according to the threshing floor technique. Ruth was to go down to the threshing floor in the evening, but she was not to make herself known. The great crowd, the excitement, the cover of darkness, and her change in the manner of dress would all contribute toward accomplishing this. She was to observe Boaz when he finished the late repast and lay down for the night on the threshing floor. It must be noted that the threshing floor was a public place, and that these incidents all took place in the open. Both men and women were lying about the threshing floor. Entire families were gathered there. There was not much privacy connected with such circumstances; but it was the custom of the day and was not considered immodest or even questionable. It was a happy family-gathering in the spirit of a religious festival. All this was at Naomi's suggestion, and she would never have suggested anything that would have compromised her daughter-in-law. Ruth was merely following the instructions of Naomi in all this. We may be sure that neither Naomi nor Ruth were doing anything indiscreet; and that if they had, it would not have received the approbation of Boaz. His wholehearted approval and complimentary speech to Ruth for her method of procedure removes any appearance of evil from the whole affair.

Ruth was instructed to go to the place where Boaz had retired, and to take her place at his feet. There she was to pull his long mantle, the *Chudda,* over her that he might know that she sought shelter and protection. This was a symbolic and modest way of telling Boaz that she would be willing to accept him as the *goel* to take Mahlon's place in a levirate marriage. Ruth could have gone before the elders of the city and demanded that he do it, and she would have been within her legal rights. But the method adopted by her, at the suggestion of Naomi, was a quiet and reticent manner of proceeding. It was so interpreted by Boaz, as we shall see.

If there is any criticism of this rather audacious method, certainly Naomi must bear the brunt of it, as it was entirely her plan. Many see no good in this plan at all. Trapp says, "It was a bold expedient but not necessarily the worse because of that." Thomson censures Naomi for not "abstaining from all appearance of evil." Others look upon it as forcing providence upon a too perilous artifice. However, others look upon this plan in a favorable way, as we have suggested beforehand. The circumstances and the period of time must be taken into consideration in judging the plan.

Ruth was obedient to Naomi in this matter, and she fulfilled every direction. In the middle of the night, Boaz became restless and turned upon his pallet. As he did, he discovered someone at his feet, and upon closer investigation, he found out that it was a woman. In the darkness, he made inquiry as to her identity. The answer of Ruth to his question is notable: "I am Ruth thine handmaid: spread therefore thy skirt over thine handmaid; for thou art a near kinsman" (Ruth 3:9). Instead of bringing him before the public eye and forcing him to perform the part of a *goel*, she was quietly giving him the opportunity of rejecting or accepting the office of *goel*. We may be sure that Naomi and Ruth would not have prosecuted the case further. They would not have embarrassed him publicly, or forced him legally to do that which he had no mind and heart to perform. But Naomi and Ruth had every provocation to believe that he was waiting to seize upon the opportunity to act as *goel* when the opportunity presented itself to him. Instead of being indecorous in this plan, they were adopting the utmost discretion and consideration. Ruth called upon Boaz to perform the duty of a *goel*. She was entirely within her rights, according to the Mosaic injunction; and in all this, she had not removed herself from the bounds of propriety. Boaz was a *goel*, and as such, he had a duty to perform.

In a later chapter, we shall consider three meanings of the Hebrew word *goel*. There is a fourth meaning that Gesenius gives for *goel* which bears upon the action of this chapter. When a man died, it was the office of the next of kin to marry his widow. We have previously quoted this law as given in the twenty-fifth chapter of Deuteronomy. When Ruth called Boaz a near kinsman, she frankly was asking him to perform the duty of a *goel*. It must be carefully observed that Ruth was not approaching a stranger in this way, and that she was not forcing this claim upon the other kinsman who had manifested no interest. She was revealing her willingness to a kinsman, who had given every token of evidence that he was desirous of performing the office of a *goel*. When she asked Boaz to spread his skirt over her, and when she called him a near kinsman, she was using a figure of speech that was tantamount to the acceptance of a marriage proposal. It was the Eastern way, in that day, of saying, "Yes, I will marry you." This is further accentuated by one of the prophets. "Now when I passed by thee, and looked upon thee, behold, thy time was the time of love; and I spread my skirt over thee, and covered thy nakedness: yea, I sware unto thee, and entered into a covenant with thee, saith the Lord God, and thou becamest mine" (Ezekiel 16:8).

The response of Boaz to Ruth revealed that he so interpreted her language. He complimented her for the expeditious and sagacious manner in which she had conducted herself. He blessed her—not blamed her—for the method of procedure. "And he said, Blessed be thou of the Lord, my daughter: for thou hast shewed more kindness in the latter end than at the beginning, inasmuch as thou followedst not young men, whether poor or rich. And now, my daughter, fear not; I will do to thee all that thou requirest: for all the city of my people doth know that thou art a virtuous woman. And now it is true that I am thy near kinsman: howbeit there is a kinsman nearer than I. Tarry this night, and it shall be in the morning, that if he will perform unto thee the part of a kinsman, well; let him do the kinsman's part: but if he will not do the part of a kinsman to thee, then will I do the part of a kinsman to thee, as the Lord liveth: lie down until the morning" (Ruth 3:10-13).

This speech of Boaz is noteworthy, for it shows that he, too, had been thinking along these lines. He had observed that she was not interested in the young men who wanted to marry. He probably had wondered many times if she had thought of marriage again, but her widow's weeds must have repelled any action on his part. He rejoiced to learn that she was willing for him to become the kinsman-redeemer. He recognized his duty under the Mosaic ordinance, and eagerly sought to fulfill it to its last jot and tittle.

Boaz had given this matter much careful consideration beforehand, for he immediately mentioned another kinsman who exercised a prior claim under the law. Boaz, doubtless, had thought many times of pressing his claim; but he knew of the other kinsman and that brought trepidation to his heart, and hesitation to his action. As he could not be sure about Ruth and the other kinsman, Boaz remained patiently in the background for a propitious time to move. Now that time had come. The willingness of Ruth made him resolve to push this case with all the energy and influence that he could muster. He would attempt to remove this legal obstacle which stood in his way.

Throughout the remainder of this book there is evidenced the eloquent fact that Boaz possessed a knowledge of this case which no one could have had unless he had spent much time considering its legal implications. He not only pointed out to Ruth the presence of another kinsman, but he also pointed out to the other kinsman the legal difficulty which would confront him if he married Ruth. He knew more about the other kinsman's legal status in the case than the kinsman did himself. That night was the turning point in the life of Ruth; and it was the decisive moment in the life of Boaz.

Boaz asserted himself fully and without delay to Ruth, and promised that the very next morning he would begin action on her behalf. The threshing floor to Boaz was the turning point of his life; but for the next few weeks it was to lose its glamor and the place of first importance for him. Instead of winnowing wheat, he would now try to winnow out the other kinsman, and gather into his garner some- one more precious than grain. It was praise- worthy, on the part of Boaz, to recognize the right of the other kinsman who was legally before him. Boaz had no intention of acting illegally in order to gain his heart's desire. This was commendable, but it is evident from the text that Boaz did everything that was honorable to discourage the kinsman from asserting his preferred claim.

He bade Ruth tarry until the morning but to return home before daylight so that she might not be recognized. Evidently if Boaz had rejected the overture of Ruth, either he or she would have been disgraced. She would have acted in presumption. She could have brought him before the elders of the city. If the other kinsman insisted on his prior claim, Boaz did not wish to cast any dark shadow over the character of Ruth. He exercised the utmost caution on her behalf. Bertheau pays this fine compliment to Boaz: "The modest man even in the middle of the night did not hesitate for a moment what it was his duty to do with regard to the young maiden (or rather woman) towards whom he felt already so strongly attached; he made his own personal inclinations subordinate to the traditional custom, and only when this permitted him to marry Ruth was he ready to do so. And not knowing whether she might not have to become the wife of the nearer *goel,* he was careful for her and her reputation, in order that he might hand her over unblemished to the man who had the undoubted right to claim her as his wife."

In verse fourteen, Boaz was evidently addressing his laborers when he said, "Let it not be known that a woman came into the floor." This was a prudent step on his part. Before Ruth left the next morning, he filled her veil with six measures of barley. This man was not only generous in the harvest field, but he was generous on the threshing floor. In the field Ruth had to glean, but on the threshing floor she received a generous portion of winnowed grain for which she had expended no labor. The veil was the large mantle worn by the poorer classes, and it was large enough to cover the entire body. It would have held a great deal of grain, but certainly Boaz did not fill it. The size of the measure used is not given. If it were as large as some suggest, then Ruth could not have lifted the load. The Targum says that it was over two bushels. Although we are forbidden to speculate, we may be sure that it was a generous portion.

The Authorized Version, in following the Vulgate, translates the final clause of verse fifteen, "and she went into the city." Coverdale also uses this translation, and in reading the passage, it seems the normal and easy method. However, the American Standard Version changes this quite properly to "and *he* went into the city." Ruth returned with the grain to her mother-in-law, and Boaz went into the city to prosecute his case, on behalf of the fair damsel. Both went into the city with full hearts, quickened stride and hastening steps. This slight change in the gender of the pronoun brings to our attention, by way of confirmation, the suggestion previously made, namely, that Boaz lost no time in expediting matters that would clear the way for him to marry Ruth. The eagerness of the man is clearly detected and must be carefully considered as we shall make further reference to this feature.

Ruth returned to her mother-in-law before it was yet light. Naomi did not recognize her as she approached, and called out, "Who art thou, my daughter?" Dr. James Morison sees in this question of Naomi no suggestion that Naomi did not distinguish the identity of Ruth but rather that Naomi asked knowingly, "Art thou Boaz' betrothed?" If the question of Naomi is treated as an idiom, then this evidently is the implication.

Ruth related all her experiences of that night to an interested mother-in-law. As a token of her reception by Boaz, Ruth called attention to the amount of grain she had brought back. It was evidently more than she had brought back the first day when she gleaned in the fields of Boaz, although handfuls of purpose had made it possible for her to bring back more than could otherwise be expected. Naomi was now confirmed in her thinking that her womanly intuition had been right. The outcome had demonstrated that Naomi was correct at the outset.

This chapter opened with Naomi seeking rest for Ruth, and it closes with that rest attained. We read in this last verse that Naomi did not send Ruth out on another mission to gain rest but advised her to remain at home and enjoy the rest which another had provided. "Then said she, Sit still, my daughter, until thou know how the matter will fall: for the man will not be in rest, until he have finished the thing this day" (Ruth 3:18). She told Ruth to remove all thought of restless anxiety from her heart, as another had become restless on her behalf. Boaz could not rest until he had found rest for Ruth, and she could rely absolutely upon him.

This is a rest that only a Redeemer can provide. It is the rest of redemption. After God created the heavens and the earth, Scripture instructs us that he rested. That was a creation rest. All was good and complete, and nothing needed to be done to improve it. Then man sinned, and God broke his creation rest. "His ox was in the ditch," and God began to move to get man out of the ditch of sin. From that day on, God has not rested. Christ said, "My Father worketh hitherto, and I work" (John 5:17). God will not rest until redemption is finished and sin is destroyed. Christ, as our Boaz, came down and redeemed us that we might have a redemption rest from the penalty of sin. He lives today and is busy that we might rest in his power. The redemption rest that is provided today for a lost sinner is to cease from his own works and trust his Redeemer-Kinsman to provide his rest. "There remaineth therefore a rest to the people of God. For he that is entered into his rest, he also hath ceased from his own works, as God did from his" (Hebrews 4:9,10). This is the rest that comes when we no longer trust our works, but receive his work of redemption on the cross as the penalty for our sins. Furthermore, we are instructed to rest in him daily and to commit our every problem and difficulty to him, as Peter wrote, "Casting all your care upon him; for he careth for you" (I Peter 5:7). Only in our great Redeemer is there rest for the restless heart of man from the threshing floor of this world, with its chaff, stubble and crowd.

"Reality, Reality.
Lord Jesus Christ Thou art to me.
From the spectral mist and the driving clouds,
From the shifting shadows and phantom crowds
From unreal words and unreal lives,
Where truth with falsehood feebly strives:
From the passings away, the chance and change,
Flickerings, vanishings, swift and strange,
   I turn to my glorious rest in Thee,
   Who art the grand Reality."

                        —*Frances Havergal*

CHAPTER 9

Legal Entanglements

"She stood breast-high amid the corn,
Clasped by the golden light of morn,
Like the sweetheart of the sun,
Who many a glowing kiss had won,
On her cheeks an autumn flush
Deeply ripened—such a blush
In the midst of brown was born,
Like red poppies grown with corn,
Round dark eyes her tresses fell,
Which were blackest none could tell,
But long lashes veiled a light
That had else been all too bright.
And her hat, with shady brim,
Made her tressy forehead dim;
Thus she stood amid the stocks,
Praising God with sweetest looks.
'Sure,' I said, 'Heaven did not mean
Where I reap thou should'st but glean;
Lay thy sheaf adown and come,
Share my harvest and my home.'"

From the very beginning there was a marvelous development in the status of Ruth. First, she was found in the land of Moab, a stranger from the covenants of promise, without hope and without God in the world. Next she was brought by providence into the field of Boaz, under the wings of the God of Israel. Then she was sent to the threshing floor of Boaz; and there she was seen asserting her claim for a kinsman-redeemer. Finally, in this last chapter of the Book of Ruth, she is seen as a bride for the heart of Boaz and as a mother in his home. What splendid progress! What scriptural evolution! From a very lowly beginning she was lifted to the very pinnacle of blessing. All this was made possible by a *goel* who loved her. She could indeed sing, "All the way my Saviour leads me." In this final chapter of the story of Ruth we have the outcome of the action initiated by Boaz in the preceding chapter. He set out upon the task of redeeming Ruth. Herein is given the fruit of his labors.

The first act of Boaz was to go early that morning to the gate of the city, where he stationed himself in a conspicuous place so that he might hail the unnamed kinsman as he went out of the city into his fields to harvest, or as he entered into the city from his threshing floor. Boaz eagerly awaited his passage so that he might waylay him. Presently that one came by, and Boaz greeted him as if he did not know his name. "Ho, such a one! turn aside, sit down here." That Boaz knew his name is unquestionably true, but why the record should withhold his name is an enigma. "Such a one" is surely not a

93

concrete identification. The Septuagint throws some light upon this by giving the word *Kpuoit*, which means "hidden one." The Hebrew conveys the same idea by the use of two words, the first meaning "to point out" and the second meaning "to conceal." It was the clear intention of the writer to conceal this name. The American idiom "so-and-so" corresponds more closely than any other expression. Why should the name of this kinsman be concealed? The next verse has resulted in a rather ingenious explanation, which is certainly the most satisfactory one considered: "And he turned aside, and sat down. And he took ten men of the elders of the city, and said, Sit ye down here. And they sat down" (Ruth 4:1,2).

When this anonymous kinsman turned aside and sat down, Boaz was already prepared to have the matter settled at once. Ten men had been chosen, elders of the city, to act as witnesses, and, perhaps, as a sort of supreme court. The gate of the city of that day and place corresponded to the market place and forum of the cities of the West, and in some respects is equivalent to our present-day county courthouse. Certainly Boaz was proceeding in a way that was according to law, and the final decision in this case was sealed in the manner set forth in the Hebrew statute book. We will let another continue this explanation as to the omission of the name of the unknown kinsman: "This powerless redeemer is the law. Ten witnesses are there confirming his inability to do it. These represent the Ten Commandments. The curse of the law rested upon the Moabitess for it is written, 'An Ammonite

94

or Moabite shall not enter into the congregation of the Lord; even to the tenth generation forever' (Deuteronomy 23:3). Therefore the law could not bring in Ruth, but only keep her out." This seems to be a satisfactory explanation for the concealment of the name of the nearer kinsman who bore the pseudonym "So-and-So." The name was surely known, and the withholding of it was done purposely. This thought will be developed further in a succeeding chapter.

In the presence of these witnesses, Boaz presented the case to this kinsman. The expression used by Boaz concerning what Naomi intended to do with the property is translated in such a way that it is misleading. "Naomi ... selleth a parcel of land, which was our brother Elimelech's." Actually she could not sell it, according to the Mosaic precept. "The land shall not be sold forever: for the land is mine; for ye are strangers and sojourners with me" (Leviticus 25:23). She could only sell a jubilee-estate in the property, which in most cases was less than a life-estate today. But the tense of the verb precludes the possibility that it means even that. The tense is perfect, and the meaning is "has sold." Coverdale translates it, "offers for sale." The American Revised Version retains the same translation here as the older versions. Dr. Driver says that a resolution or determination to do something in the future often required the perfect tense, and he cites this passage in Ruth as an instance of that. It seems to us that the best interpretation is offered by the *Preacher's Homiletic Commentary*, namely, that the stress and strain of the years of famine had forced Naomi to sell her property some-time subsequent to her return to Bethlehem. Dr. Elliott suggests that Elimelech had done this before he died. In any case, the land needed to be re-deemed, as adverse circumstances had forced it out of the hands of the family. When Naomi first re-turned from Moab, she was in no position to have the property turned over to her; but as the clouds began to leave her sky, she felt inclined to get the family estate back into its proper channel. It was part of the estate of Elimelech; and as he was a brother to the unnamed kinsman and to Boaz, it was their prerogative to redeem. The first to qualify was the "So-and-So" kinsman, and then Boaz, if the other refused. The term "brother" which was ap-plied to Elimelech by Boaz implied no such strict interpretation as is given the word today. It was a loose term which could refer even to a nephew or cousin. We shall show in a succeeding chapter that the kinsman with a pseudonym was a brother of Elimelech and that Boaz was a nephew of Elime-lech. The point to note here is that both men were related by blood to Elimelech, and were, therefore, *goels*.

Most commentators omit this passage, which must be detected if we are to discover the subtle method of Boaz. He did not approach the anony-mous kinsman in the same way that Ruth had approached him. She claimed her rights as a wid-ow, under the statute regarding the *goel*. She did not mention the property. Evidently Boaz had dis-cussed that angle of the case with her. When Boaz presented the case to this unnamed kinsman, he made the property the important issue. There was a clear change of tactics on the part of Boaz. He mentioned first a *goel* for the property, and then presented the case of a *goel* for Ruth, as a last alternative to deter this kinsman. The change of emphasis that was made by Boaz is essential in revealing the eagerness of this man to have Ruth for his wife. The kinsman expressed a willingness to redeem when he thought it only involved the property, but Boaz was prepared to present the supreme difficulty in order to discourage him. Boaz was certainly tending to this matter speedily, expeditiously and righteously, but he was also using some of the wisdom of the serpent. He raised this final objection as a natural barrier, which was destined to cause this kinsman to relinquish all claims. "Then said Boaz, What day thou buyest the field of the hand of Naomi, thou must buy it also of Ruth the Moabitess, the wife of the dead, to raise up the name of the dead upon his inheritance" (Ruth 4:5).

That which Ruth presented as the foremost claim for a kinsman-redeemer, Boaz reserved last, as a climax. Ruth had a claim upon the estate of Elimelech. The two sons of Elimelech were the natural heirs to the estate. If either one had left a son, he would have been the natural heir to the estate. They did not leave a child; so, their wives could pass the estate on to any child born to them by a kinsman-redeemer of the family of Elimelech. Delitzsch and Kiel explain the legal side of this affair, which took place at the city gate, in this way: "So far as the fact itself was concerned, the field, which Naomi had sold from want, was the hereditary property of her deceased husband, and ought therefore to descend to her sons according to the standing rule of right; and in this respect, therefore, it was Ruth's property quite as much as Naomi's. From the negotiations between Boaz and the nearer redeemer, it is very evident that Naomi had sold the field which was the hereditary property of her husband, and was lawfully entitled to sell it. But as landed property did not descend to wives according to the Israelitish law, but only to children, and when there were no children, to the nearest relatives of the husband (Numbers 27:8-11), when Elimelech died his field properly descended to his sons; and when they died without children, it ought to have passed to his nearest relations. Hence the question arises, what right had Naomi to sell her husband's field as her own property?"

There is a technical problem here that is made more difficult because of the lack of sufficient data on other cases in Israel. Although it seems clear that neither Naomi nor Ruth could dispose of the property of the estate of Elimelech, yet both possessed certain rights in it. They were able by birth to convey the title of the property to their sons. Ruth's son by Boaz is called by the women of the city the "kinsman-redeemer of Naomi." Such he was, for he inherited the estate of Elimelech, the husband of Naomi. He did not inherit it from Ruth, Naomi or Boaz, but from them he received the title to it. Ruth was the only one who could raise up a son to inherit the estate of Elimelech. Therefore, she was not only an important link in the chain of genealogy but she sustained certain rights over the property which Boaz was discussing with the other kinsman. To redeem the property, therefore, would involve the *goel* in the affairs of the foreigner from Moab. The one who redeemed the estate would have to redeem Ruth also, as she and her affairs were bound up in the field of Elimelech, legally. This was the legal technicality upon which Boaz was depending for his victory.

When the attention of Mr. "So-and-So" was called to this serious difficulty possessing legal implications, he declared that he could not redeem the stranger of Moab without involving his own estate: "And the kinsman said, I cannot redeem it for myself, lest I mar mine own inheritance: redeem thou my right to thyself; for I cannot redeem it" (Ruth 4:6).

The Targum states that he had a wife and child, which fact would cause a marriage with the Gentile girl to jeopardize their interests. Lange infers that it was merely superstition on his part, as Ruth was associated with the extinguishment of one estate.

The more normal interpretation to place upon his words appears to be that the presence of the Moabitess as an inescapable appurtenance to the property aroused in his mind fears concerning a clear title to any estate in which anyone who was condemned in such unmistakable terms by the Mosaic system (Deuteronomy 23:3) had an interest. This law prevented a Moabite from entering the congregation, even to the tenth generation. It was this law, so it seems, that prevented him from prosecuting his preferred claim. He was evidently frightened by the presence of Ruth, and he immediately surrendered his rights as a redeemer to Boaz.

As further evidence that this agreement between Boaz and the other kinsman was accomplished in a legal manner, the method by which they sealed the bargain presents irrefutable proofs. In order to make a contract or agreement binding, it was necessary to follow an unusual procedure. The law was given in Deuteronomy 25:7-9, in connection with a case to which this one of Ruth's was similar. It is repeated in the last chapter of Ruth, with a few minor omissions. "Now this was the manner in former time in Israel concerning redeeming and concerning changing, for to confirm all things; a man plucked off his shoe, and gave it to his neighbour:, and this was a testimony in Israel" (verse 7). The removal of the shoe, and the placing of it in the hands of the party of the first part was a legal document of great significance in that day. In the law in Deuteronomy there is mention made that when the kinsman-redeemer refused to marry the widow of the deceased, she was to take the shoe from off his foot and, also, to spit in his face. The man who refused to perform the part of a kinsman-redeemer was thereafter called "the house of him that hath his shoe loosed." It is easy to see why the other part of the law did not survive. Boaz did not spit in the man's face, but he did draw off his shoe. Another detail that is worth noting is that this action was to be performed by the widow, and in this instance it should have been Ruth. Boaz was acting for Ruth in this case. In view of the fact that she was a Gentile, and that she was too modest to push the matter publicly, Boaz acted in her place and on her behalf. This fact is usually overlooked.

Boaz now possessed the shoe of the anonymous kinsman, which was in one sense his marriage license, for it was a legal document, bearing all the seals of a court order. This kinsman, who has not borne a name up to the present, must now be dubbed with the euphemistic nickname, "Barefoot." It is a name of reproach. Henceforth he is a "barefoot" redeemer.

This "barefoot" redeemer represents the law, and is unable to redeem the sinner, for Scripture says, "For what the law could not do, in that it was weak through the flesh." The law is barefoot, as far as the sinner is concerned, for it cannot clothe him or put shoes on his feet. It is the gospel of grace that clothes a sinner in the righteousness of Christ and puts shoes on his feet. "And your feet shod with the preparation of the gospel of peace" (Ephesians 6:15). The law cannot redeem and must retreat in shame and disgrace, but Christ, our Boaz, can redeem in grace.

With the legal document in his possession, the shoe of "barefoot," Boaz concluded the transaction by calling the ten elders to witness that he now was the one who had that day redeemed the estate of Elimelech, Mahlon and Chilion. Not only was he the redeemer of the estate, but he was the kinsman-redeemer of Ruth. "Moreover Ruth the Moabitess, the wife of Mahlon, have I purchased to be my wife, to raise up the name of the dead upon his inheritance, that the name of the dead be not cut off from among his brethren, and from the gate of his place: ye are witnesses this day" (Ruth 4:10).

What far-reaching consequences that transaction was to have! The immediate accomplishments seem unspeakable. It changed the status of two very sad and poor widows. It made one of them a bride and a mother, and it lifted the veil of bitterness from the other and made her truly Naomi—"pleasant." It lifted Boaz out of the commonplace existence of a monotonous farmer's life, which he was living alone, into the realm of great blessing and joy. It paved the way for David and, ultimately, for Christ.

Before the close of the day which had begun so auspiciously, Boaz had concluded all his work of a kinsman-redeemer. He became the bridegroom-redeemer. Walter Baxendale calls attention to a very interesting fact about this transaction. It was concluded with prayer by the elders of the city. Here is one of the prayers of Scripture which is not so classified: "And all the people that were in the gate, and the elders, said, We are witnesses. The Lord make the woman that is come into thine house like Rachel and like Leah, which two did build the house of Israel: and do thou worthily in Ephratah, and be famous in Bethlehem: and let thy house be like the house of Pharez, whom Tamar bare unto Judah, of the seed which the Lord shall give thee of this young woman" (Ruth 4:11,12).

The business transaction and the marriage were concluded with prayer. Just as business is not solely a secular affair divorced from God, neither is marriage separated from the life of God. Marriages

102

are made in heaven, and if not, they become an earthly hell. This entire story illustrates the great truth that God is profoundly interested in the love of men and women for each other, when it blossoms forth into a happy marriage which has his blessing.

Ruth was the sole object that prompted Boaz to conclude this business with such alacrity and expediency. His love for the young maid of Moab afforded him sufficient reason to become the kinsman-redeemer. The story concludes quite properly with the succinct statement, "So Boaz took Ruth, and she was his wife." This is the happy ending of every good story. God places in the heart of a man love and affection for a woman, and he makes that feeling mutual. It is his divine intention that they be united in marriage, in his presence, with his blessing invoked upon the union. The divorce of marriage from the plan of God, as if it were something with which he took no interest, or of which he heartily disapproved, is detrimental to marriage and unfair to God. When marriage is alienated from the plan of God, it ends always in divorce.

The happy marriage of Boaz and Ruth illustrates the glorious ending of the earthly career of the Church, when she will be removed from this world and brought into his presence, where she will be united to Christ in marriage. "Let us be glad and rejoice, and give honour to him: for the marriage of the Lamb is come, and his wife hath made herself ready" (Revelation 19:7). The Church will someday be united to Christ as the redeemed Gentile bride of the Lamb.

"Love he sent to bind
The disunited tendrils of that vine
Which bears the wine of life, the human heart."

However, there is another chapter to our story which, although it is not meant to contribute to its beauty, does contribute to one of the supreme objectives. The remainder of chapter four tells of the birth of Obed to Ruth and Boaz. This gives occasion for the inclusion of the great genealogy at the end. This genealogy is transferred, in its entirety, to the opening of the New Testament in the Gospel of Matthew. It sets forth the incidents of this humble story as a link in the great plan and purpose of God. The birth of Obed to Ruth and Boaz at Bethlehem shadows forth the birth of Another, whose coming was to reverberate to the ends of the earth and to have ecumenical and eternal effect upon this world.

The name Obed means "servant" or "worshiper." The women of Bethlehem named him in his relationship to Naomi. Although he was of no blood kin to Naomi, he was legally her grandson. He was a little servant to Naomi in her old age, and took the place left vacant by the death of a husband and two sons. Now her estate would go to the little servant. This one who was the offspring of a Moabitess was a worshiper of the true God, even as his mother.

The Book of Ruth, coming from the times of the judges, is like a lovely flower in a weed patch. The fragrance of this story has been wafted by the winds to the farthest corner of the earth.

CHAPTER 10

It's the Law

In most works on redemption, very little attention, if any, is given to the person of the redeemer.
Consequently, the Book of Ruth is ignored, for the
person of the redeemer is of primary importance in
this narrative. Jonathan Edwards, in tracing the
history of redemption from Moses to David, absolutely ignores Boaz as a type of Christ, the great
Redeemer. He mentions many of the judges in this
commendatory language: "The deliverers that God
raised up from time to time were all types of Christ,
the great Redeemer of his Church; and some of
them very remarkably so; as particularly, Barak,
Jephthah, Gideon, Samson, in many particulars."
Having included Samson, he passes over the Book
of Ruth entirely, pays no attention to Boaz, and

discusses Samuel as the next in order as a type of the Redeemer. Strong, in his *Systematic Theology*, defines the section of theology under "Christology" as "the redemption wrought by Christ," and he does not even allude to Boaz as a type of Christ. There is no reference to the Book of Ruth in his entire work on theology. Calvin, in the *Institutes*, makes no reference to the Book of Ruth when contemplating redemption. In any Biblical history of redemption that seeks to trace the types through the Scripture, there ought to be a reference to Boaz in the Book of Ruth.

The entire scheme of scriptural redemption is deposited upon the person of a redeemer. The redeemer is essential to any satisfactory system of redemption. In the Book of Ruth, the person of the redeemer is fully illustrated in the person of Boaz. He is the only example of a Hebrew *goel* in the Old Testament. Boaz was the kinsman-redeemer and is "the plain figure of Christ." Naomi identified Boaz as the *goel* (kinsman-redeemer, Ruth 2:20) of their family.

The Hebrew *goel* is translated by the English word "kinsman" (Ruth 3:9), and by the word "redeemer" (Job 19:25). Probably the best translation which combines both thoughts is "kinsman-redeemer." Simply stated, the word means "to set free." Gesenius gives three meanings for the root word which define the different aspects of the word:

1. To redeem, buy back. The simple thought is to purchase by paying a price for that which was lost by some reason.

106

2. To require blood, *i. e.*, to avenge bloodshed. This had reference to someone who was near of kin, as only such a one would seek vengeance.
3. "Since both the right of redemption (1) and the office of avenging bloodshed (2) belonged to the nearest kinsman, this Hebrew word denotes near of kin, near relative."

There are two thoughts in this word which the various meanings suggest. The first refers to the person of the redeemer. The redeemer must be a kinsman. This requires the redeemer to be a blood relation, and if he is unable to meet this stipulation, he forfeits all legitimate claims to the title. This is of tremendous importance, in consideration of the blood redemption for the sinner provided by Christ. Not only did he shed his blood; but it was the blood of one who was blood-kin to us. Even on the human plane, not every person could qualify as a redeemer for another. The person of the redeemer is uppermost in any consideration of redemption.

The second thought in the Hebrew word *goel* refers to the process of redeeming. Redemption may refer either to the person, or property, or both. A person who has sold himself or who has been sold into slavery can be redeemed by a kinsman. The property of a person can be redeemed by a kinsman. He can recover from penalty both the person and the property, recovering the property to the rightful owner, and restoring the person to a place of freedom. If a man, through misfortune or untoward circumstances, was forced to mortgage his property, and then was unable to recover it at the date of maturity of the mortgage, the property passed into the hands of the mortgager until the "year of jubilee." In any period during that interval, a kinsman of the mortgagee could pay the mortgage and restore the property to the rightful owner. This same thing applied to the person himself. If he did not have any property, he could sell himself into slavery. The kinsman could, at any time, restore him to freedom by paying the sum required to meet the debt. The *goel* could move into civil court and recover the property, and he could go into criminal court and deliver the person from the penalty of the law. We see that only a kinsman could perform this peculiar, but withal vital, work for a poor relation.

The second meaning of the term *goel* does not figure in this consideration of redemption as it is in no way connected with the Book of Ruth. There is, however, a thought in it that we wish to indicate at this time in connection with the kinsman-redeemer. This is mentioned in connection with the cities of refuge where a man could flee if he killed another person accidentally. Here, he was to be protected from the *goel* of the man he had inadvertently slain. The close blood kin of the murdered man would want revenge, and the slayer would be protected in that event. If the slaying were premeditated, and the murderer intentionally killed another, it was allowed under the law for a *goel* to take revenge, by slaying him in turn. This was the expressed language of the code of Israel: "The revenger [*goel*] of blood himself shall slay the murderer: when he meeteth him, he shall slay him" (Numbers 35:19).

This aspect of the meaning of the *goel* was wonderfully fulfilled in Christ. Sin and Satan have killed man and are therefore murderers. Satan is called a murderer in Scripture, and man is his victim. In the Garden of Eden he led man to eat of that which brought death to the human family. Sin today is a partner in the crime, for "the wages of sin is death." And Paul speaks of sin as an actual murderer. "For sin, taking occasion by the commandment, deceived me, and by it slew me" (Romans 7:11).

The law is the third party to the unholy trinity. The law is not evil in itself, but it is a horrible taskmaster. "For I was alive without the law once: but when the commandment came, sin revived, and I died" (Romans 7:9). Man must be redeemed from the law also for it has become innocently a partner in the crime of murdering the human race. Man had no kinsman to avenge him of this dastardly deed, but the Saviour was promised who would be an enemy of Satan and his destroyer: "And I will put enmity between thee and the woman, and between thy seed and her seed; it shall bruise thy head, and thou shalt bruise his heel" (Genesis 3:15).

In the fullness of time, the avenger of blood came that "through death he might destroy him that had the power of death, that is, the devil" (Hebrews 2:14). He came to redeem us from sin and the law. He hates sin and Satan because they have been the cause of man's undoing. As we shall presently see, Christ did not pay a ransom to the devil, but he did ransom us from the power of the devil. Christ, in dealing with Satan and sin, is the avenger of the blood kinsman. Our Redeemer loved us when we were dead in sin, but he hated sin and Satan.

God is seen in Scripture as the Redeemer of both persons and property. God told Moses that he would be the Kinsman-Redeemer of Israel. He identified himself as the *Goel* of these people. "I will redeem you with a stretched out arm" (Exodus 6:6). He redeemed their persons from the slavery of Egypt, but he likewise was the redeemer of their property. The gifts that they made to the construction of the Tabernacle in the wilderness reveal that they left Egypt a rich nation. That did not conclude God's redemption of these people. He was not only redeeming them from Egypt but he promised to deliver them into the land pledged to Abraham. "And I will bring you in unto the land, concerning the which I did swear to give it to Abraham" (Exodus 6:8). The redemption included the land. God was the *Goel* of both their persons and their property.

In the Book of Ruth there is an instance of each of these aspects of redemption. There is, primarily, a redemption of the property of Elimelech, but the *goel* in this particular case had to redeem the maid from Moab, according to the penal code in Deuteronomy 25:5-10. The *goel*, as a near kinsman, had to marry the widow of the deceased to raise up the name of the brother. There could have been no redemption of the property of Elimelech without a redemption of Ruth, as Boaz clearly indicated in his answer to the "barefoot" kinsman: "Then said Boaz, What day thou buyest the field of the hand of

110

Naomi, thou must buy it also of Ruth the Moabitess, the wife of the dead, to raise up the name of the dead upon his inheritance" (Ruth 4:5).

The refusal of the "barefoot" kinsman to redeem the property, if it involved the redemption of the person of the Gentile girl, abundantly confirms that both must be done, and that there could be no separation of the person and the property.

Boaz qualified as a bona fide kinsman-redeemer. He was a blood relation of Elimelech. He was willing to redeem, and he was able to redeem. He was free from any involvement or entanglement that would compromise his person, position or property. Boaz was a capable redeemer who was potentially endowed with all the qualifications that could be asked of him in this function. As such, he is a worthy figure of Christ, who is greater than Boaz. The credentials of Boaz will be examined in the next few chapters. We are stressing here the first thought concerning the word *goel*, that is, the person who acts as a redeemer must meet every specification, for the entire structure of redemption rests upon him.

In order to make clear in our minds God's method of redeeming, it will be necessary to examine the method by which property and persons were redeemed under the Mosaic system. In a preceding chapter we have made reference to the marriage of a widow, which was a redemption for her, according to Deuteronomy 25:5-10. The law concerning the redemption of property is stated in the following way: "And in all the land of your possession ye shall grant a redemption for the land. If thy brother

111

be waxen poor, and hath sold away some of his possession, and if any of his kin come to redeem it, then shall he redeem that which his brother sold" (Leviticus 25:24,25).

There were two things that were true regarding all real estate in Israel. First of all, God was the owner; and the inhabitants had no such relation to the land. God carefully instructed them in this great fact: "The land shall not be sold forever: for the land is mine; for ye are strangers and sojourners with me" (Leviticus 25:23). The individuals were tenants upon the land. They merely rented from God. Therefore they could not finally dispose of the property. No man could grant a clear title to land, and there were no fee simple deeds. The nation, Israel, held an eternal title in the land of Canaan; but the individuals possessed only temporary rights, which were forfeited when they sinned. When God sent the entire nation into captivity, he did not abrogate the title deeds to that land, and the nation did not default in such a way as to lose their right to it. But the individuals who composed the nation at that time were removed off the land, for, after all, they had only squatter's rights, which they forfeited for sin.

The second and final thing which was true regarding real estate in Israel grows out of the first. As they were not owners of the land, they could not make a final disposition of it. It was impossible for a person to let the real estate of his family finally pass out of the hands of himself and his children. He might mortgage it, but the one who held the mortgage understood that in the "year of jubilee" the land returned to the rightful heir of the family who originally possessed it. Between the time of the mortgage and the year of jubilee it was possible for a kinsman to redeem it, by paying the mortgage and restoring the property to the family estate. It was not incumbent upon the kinsman to redeem, but the Mosaic system granted him the prerogative, if he cared to exercise it.

The other class to which redemption applied is that of persons. This phase of the law is stated in these terms: "And if a sojourner or stranger wax rich by thee, and thy brother that dwelleth by him wax poor, and sell himself unto the stranger or sojourner by thee, or to the stock of the stranger's family: after that he is sold he may be redeemed again; one of his brethren may redeem him: either his uncle, or his uncle's son, may redeem him, or any that is nigh of kin unto him of his family may redeem him; or if he be able, he may redeem himself. And he shall reckon with him that bought him from the year that he was sold to him unto the year of jubilee: and the price of his sale shall be according unto the number of years, according to the time of an hired servant shall it be with him. If there be yet many years behind, according unto them he shall give again the price of his redemption out of the money that he was bought for" (Leviticus 25:47-51).

If a man, through unfortunate or untoward circumstances, found himself in poverty, and a stranger next to him, during the same interval, had become wealthy, it was likely that the Israelite would find himself at the mercy of his rich neighbor.

He would probably find himself on the short end of a hard bargain, which would terminate in his selling himself into slavery to the rich man. This was a terrible plight for an Israelite, but it became the unhappy lot of many. In this hopeless position he would forever remain if it were not for a clause in the Mosaic law.

In the year of jubilee, every slave was freed in the land of Israel, according to this beneficent law. This year occurred only twice a century, and death might come before the year of jubilee. In that case, there was another clause which brought hope to the heart of the Israelite and redemption to his person. A *goel* could redeem him from the horrible condition of slavery. A rich kinsman, in such a time and under such circumstances, must have been a wonderful deliverer to an Israelite, for the *goel* could break the shackles of slavery. The *goel* was a savior for every Israelite in slavery.

Another important feature of the general subject of redemption is found in the legal tender of redemption. The legal tender of redemption was the coin used in any business transaction. The *goel* paid for the release of the property and person with the money that would have been required in any transaction. In other words, the *goel* had to have the *price* of redemption.

In this same connection, the nation, Israel, was a redeemed people. In what sense were they a redeemed people? The answer that is commonly given to this question is rather stereotyped. They were redeemed by blood and power. The blood of the Passover lamb marked the first stage of their redemption. The death angel passed over the land of Egypt; and in every home where there was not the blood upon the doorposts and lintel, he smote the firstborn of man and beast. The blood on the entrance of the home kept the angel of death on the outside, and he passed over. The occupants therein partook of the feast that night in joy, and afterwards passed out of the land of Egypt. In the midst of the sorrow of Egypt, they went out rejoicing. They were delivered from death. They were redeemed by blood. That was the first coin of redemption.

The Red Sea blocked their exodus from Egypt. The Egyptians were pursuing them in order to slay them. Again, God became their redeemer, but the type of exchange used was different. With mighty power he opened the Red Sea so that they might cross dry-shod. This marked the second stage of redemption, but it does not exhaust the truth concerning Israel's redemption. Up to this point, the people of Israel were only freed slaves, and a motley mob they were. They were not prepared to worship God. Redemption is not complete until it brings a lost sinner from the slavery of Egypt into the presence of the holy God. The lost sinner must be given a heart with which to worship, and he must be individually redeemed. It was necessary, therefore, for each Israelite to pay the price of his redemption, even from the poorest to the richest, about twenty years old and upward. This was the law. "And the Lord spake unto Moses, saying, When thou takest the sum of the children of Israel after their number, then shall they give every man a ransom for his soul unto the Lord, when thou numberest them; that there be no plague among them, when thou numberest them. This they shall give, every one that passeth among them that are numbered, half a shekel after the shekel of the sanctuary: (a shekel is twenty gerahs) an half shekel shall be the offering of the Lord. The rich shall not give more, and the poor shall not give less than half a shekel, when they give an offering unto the Lord, to make an atonement for your souls" (Exodus 30:11-13,15).

The thirtieth chapter of Exodus is the great worship chapter of the Hebrew economy. A peculiar kind of redemption was required by those who worshiped God, and it was paid by the Israelite himself. This constituted a sort of poll tax which reminded him that he had been redeemed with a price. Israel was redeemed by blood, power and a price. The price was the payment of the silver half shekel. Redemption always involved the payment of a price. There could be no redemption in Israel without the payment of the stipulated price. Therefore, redemption required that the redeemer be able to pay the price.

This is further emphasized in the redemption of persons and property. In the case of property, the price of redemption was measured in money, or something of value which was in turn measured by money. In the case of persons, the price was measured always in terms of money. Redemption always involved the payment of a price. There were three essential characteristics of redemption which were vital to its accomplishment. Redemption required that there be a redeemer, a *goel*—one who was a kinsman. The next requirement was the method of redeeming. Property or a person could be redeemed only under certain conditions. Finally, the redeemer had to have the price of redemption. Each of these requirements of the Hebrew *goel* was included in the very word itself. If any one of these were absent, then there was no *goel* (*e.g.*, a man might have been a brother to some poor slave, but if he did not have the price of redemption, he was not a *goel*).

These three features of the *goel* demonstrate conclusively that the whole doctrine of redemption rests upon one foundation and that is the Redeemer himself. "For other foundation can no man lay than that is laid, which is Jesus Christ" (I Corinthians 3:11). The "kinsman-redeemer" is the hope of the sinner. There is no redemption for him without Christ. Strong is correct in declaring that Christology is redemption and redemption is Christology. We shall consider the subject of redemption in connection with the person of the redeemer.

There are five facts concerning the person of the redeemer which must be true, or else he cannot qualify as a legitimate redeemer under God's program:

1. The redeemer must be a near kinsman.
2. The redeemer must perform in willingness his work of redemption.
3. The redeemer must possess the ability to redeem.
4. The redeemer must be free himself.

5. The redeemer must have the price of redemption.

Boaz met all of these qualifications in the case concerning Ruth. He is but a type, and Christ is the antitype. All of these find their final and complete fulfillment in Christ. In his humanity, he met the first two qualifications. In his deity, he fulfilled the next two requirements. As the God-man, he met the final qualification. We shall examine each one of these requirements in a separate chapter. First, we shall consider each in its relationship and fulfillment in the Book of Ruth; and then we shall see how this adumbrates Christ. Boaz met all of these requirements for Ruth and became her kinsman-redeemer who satisfies the heart of every redeemed sinner. We have a Kinsman-Redeemer who satisfies the heart of every redeemed sinner, and who meets all his needs.

> "I will sing of my Redeemer,
> And his wondrous love to me;
> On the cruel cross he suffered,
> From the curse to set me free.

> "I will tell the wondrous story,
> How my lost estate to save,
> In his boundless love and mercy,
> He the ransom freely gave."

CHAPTER 11

Close Relative

"O God, O kinsman loved but not enough!
   O man, with eyes majestic after death,
Whose feet have toiled along our pathways rough,
   Whose lips drawn human breath!
By that one likeness which is ours and thine,
By that one nature which doth hold us kin;
By that high heavens where sinless thou dost shine,
   To draw us sinners in."

Anselm, in *Cur Deus Homo*, reduces to one
well-defined point the problem of why God became
a man. That point is defined by one word: redemption. The Word was made flesh in order to pay the
ransom for man's sin. John the Baptist called the
Word "the Lamb of God, which taketh away the sin
of the world." His problem resolves itself into the

119

declaration that the redeemer must be a near kinsman.

In the first verse of chapter two of Ruth, Boaz is first mentioned as a kinsman of Naomi. This word does not designate the *goel* but is a term that probably does not even suggest blood relationship. It can mean no more than acquaintance. But when Naomi spoke of Boaz as a kinsman in verse twenty of the same chapter, the word *goel* was employed. In order that it might not become an ambiguous word, she prefaced this name with the following: "The man is near of kin unto us, one of our next kinsmen [*goel*]." The difference in the usage of the two terms to describe the relationship between Boaz and the family of Elimelech is explained in the meaning of the word *goel*. In the first verse, the writer of this book is making a general statement regarding Boaz. He actually was no blood relation of Naomi, and the first word helps to keep that clear. *Goel* is a technical term and is employed by Naomi to designate the position of Boaz in relationship to them. Although he was no blood relation of either Naomi or Ruth, he stood in the place of a *goel* because of his kinship to Elimelech. In the first verse the statement is made that he was "of the family of Elimelech." This is an indefinite generalization. In verse twenty, Naomi says that he is "near of kin unto us." Technically, he was in the position of a kinsman-redeemer because of his blood relationship to Elimelech. It was the family estate of Elimelech that was in need of a redeemer. It was the widow of a son of Elimelech who was in need of a redeemer. Boaz was this *goel* because of blood connection; he was in this technical position of a *goel* because of his blood tie with the family of Elimelech.

Boaz recognized that he was a kinsman-redeemer for these two widows, for he gladly made the acknowledgment, "And now it is true that I am thy near kinsman." Boaz never denied this technical position which he occupied by blood. Just what the relationship of Boaz to the family of Elimelech was problematical, but Scripture affords us some suggestions. When the definite relationship of the *goel* was given, that there might be some order followed, the uncle of the man who needed to be redeemed exercised seniority, and then next, the son of the uncle or the cousin of the man who needed to be redeemed. After these two, any kinsman could step forward and assert his claim (Leviticus 25:49). Boaz mentioned another kinsman who was nearer than he. The implication is that the "barefoot" kinsman was a brother of Elimelech. Boaz was evidently a third brother, and therefore, a nephew of the other kinsman and of Elimelech. This would mean that he was a cousin of Mahlon, the first husband of Ruth. Kiel and Delitzsch confirm this position by stating: "According to the rabbinical tradition, which is not well established however, Boaz was a nephew of Elimelech."

In speaking to the "barefoot" kinsman who was nearer than he, Boaz recognized that he did not have the first claim, but that the other kinsman had prior rights. Boaz acknowledged that "I am after thee." In speaking to the anonymous kinsman concerning Elimelech, Boaz called him "our brother

Elimelech's." Both of these men were *goels* for the estate of Elimelech, with Boaz in second position. The other had legal precedence.

The presence of this other kinsman, and his primary rights as a kinsman, demands attention. The only fact that is stated concerning him is that he was a nearer kinsman than Boaz. Although he retained a superior claim and was willing to redeem, apparently he did not have the ability to consummate the act of redeeming, with Ruth in the case, without endangering his private estate. His willingness was not the eagerness which characterized Boaz, for Boaz apparently endangered his inheritance when he married Ruth (Deuteronomy 23:3). If he did, he was able to overcome any existing barriers. The "barefoot" kinsman lacked any intention of playing the part of the kinsman-redeemer until reminded by Boaz; and then, when the danger involved was pointed out to him, he withdrew his generous offer in a state of alarm. He was frightened away by the presence of the Gentile girl. On the other hand, she was the magnetic power which attracted Boaz, and the withdrawal of the claims of the other kinsman paved the way for Boaz to become the *goel*. Boaz was the *goel* per se, but it was necessary for the other kinsman to retire in his behalf.

When Boaz went down to the gate of the city of Bethlehem, he sat down to wait for the coming of the anonymous kinsman through the gate. This was more than a convenient place to locate the kinsman; otherwise Boaz would have gone to his home to wait. The gate was the place where contracts were made legal. The procedure of Boaz was equivalent to that which occurs today when a notary public attaches his seal to a document to make it binding in a court of law. The city gate of an Eastern city was similar in many respects to the present-day courthouse. Stone benches were placed there for the accommodation of the crowd, and the gateway became a market place and a forum. Ten elders of the city were summoned. These men evidently sat upon these stone benches when they gave legal advice in reference to problems of law which arose from time to time. The elders were apparently already present at the gate, for that represented their place of business. These men acted, in this case, as witnesses, judges and attorneys. If it had been necessary to have an opinion rendered in this case, these judges would have done it. In the event of any disagreement, they would have handed down a decision.

Boaz notified the other kinsman that Naomi was going to sell part of the estate of Elimelech. It is apparent that there had been a consultation beforehand between either Boaz and Ruth or between Boaz and Naomi. Perhaps Naomi had instructed Ruth to inform Boaz privately of the financial affairs of the family. Boaz gleaned this information in confidence, and wanted to pass it on in the same way, as his speech with the other kinsman indicates: "I thought to advertise thee." This reflects very unfavorably upon Boaz, for a more literal rendering has it, "I will uncover thine ear." Our idiom corresponding to this is: "I will whisper it in your ear." It was the financial condition of Naomi that he had learned in private. It was not ready for publication until a kinsman was ready to act upon it, and then necessity forced it to be made public. "Buy it before the inhabitants, and before the elders of my people."

Then Boaz acknowledged the right of this unknown kinsman to redeem, and graciously admitted him to his legal right. "If thou wilt redeem it, redeem it." The remainder of this legal transaction brought out the inability of this kinsman to redeem, under the extraordinary conditions which existed in this case. This kinsman was not willing to expose himself to any legal difficulty. Boaz alone was willing to pay the price which made him the only competent kinsman-redeemer of the estate and of Ruth.

The redemption of the estate involved the redemption of Ruth, the Moabitess. The presence of Ruth cast a dark shadow over the entire transaction, for she was the widow of Mahlon, and the only one, at this time, who could raise up an heir for the estate. Nevertheless, the Mosaic law rejected Ruth, and not only treated her as an outsider but kept her from enjoying the covenant relation which the nation Israel possessed (Deuteronomy 23:3). The *goel* who redeemed the property had to redeem her. There was no other alternative. She was rejected until there could be found one who was willing to pay the price.

Boaz was the only one who would pay the price. Boaz was the kinsman-redeemer in a twofold manner: he was a near kinsman by blood relation, and he was a redeemer by exclusion. The presence of

124

Ruth excluded the other kinsman. Boaz occupied a unique position.

This story, on the human plane, finds full fruition in Christ who is greater than Boaz. The Lord Jesus Christ is the great kinsman-redeemer. Job's heart-cry finds perfect fulfillment in him. "I know that my redeemer liveth, and that he shall stand at the latter day upon the earth." Boaz is the only kinsman-redeemer who is a type of Christ as our kinsman-redeemer. Boaz occupied a peculiar place in reference to Ruth and Naomi. Christ occupies a unique place in reference to man.

When the covenant of redemption was under consideration, the Son, the Second Person of the Godhead, agreed to come to this earth and provide a redemption for lost sinners in the very place where God had permitted sin to enter. When the covenant of redemption was in the process of fulfillment, Christ did not resort to any of the theophanies or Christophanies of the Old Testament. He did not come as "the angel of the Lord" or "the angel of the covenant," but "we see Jesus, who was made a little lower than the angels for the suffering of death" (Hebrews 2:9). When the redemption of man engaged the attention of the Godhead, "God sent forth his Son, made of a woman, made under the law, to redeem them that were under the law" (Galatians 4:4,5).

Christ became a man. God appeared in the tent of human flesh. The Son took upon himself the form of a servant. The one who was in the *morphe* of God was made in the similitude of man. Christ, who is the image of the invisible God, became a visible man that all might behold his glory. God created man in the image of God and that was the consummation of the work of creation. God took upon himself the likeness of man and that was the initiation of the work of redemption. When man, the creature, sinned, God did not withdraw from man; but he came down first to seek the sinner, and finally he came down in the likeness of sinful flesh to redeem the sinner.

In the Garden of Eden, man sought to be like God and failed. In the sinful world, Christ sought to become like man and succeeded. He came down where we were and got close to us. God became kin to us that he might redeem us. One of the identifying marks of the sons of Adam is death. "As in Adam all die." They are all made of the same flesh and cast in the same mold. "Christ died" is another way of saying that he was a son of Adam, and as such, he is kin to the race of man and is a part of the human family. "Forasmuch then as the children are partakers of flesh and blood, he also himself likewise took part of the same; that through death he might destroy him that had the power of death, that is, the devil; and deliver them who through fear of death were all their lifetime subject to bondage. For verily he took not on him the nature of angels; but he took on him the seed of Abraham" (Hebrews 2:14-16).

In the genealogy in Luke's Gospel, Christ's lineage is traced to Adam, the father of the race (3:38). After the flesh, Christ was a son of Adam. In addition, the writer to the Hebrews mentions that "he took on him the seed of Abraham." The genealogy, which opens the New Testament in the Gospel of Matthew, declares in the first verse that Christ was the son of David and the son of Abraham. As a son of David, he is related to the nation of Israel. As a son of Adam, he is related to the Gentiles. As a son of Abraham, he is related to the believers in the Church. Abraham was not racially a Jew, although he was the father of that race. He is not any more a Jew than he is an Arab, or an Ishmaelite, for he was the father of all three nations. He was a Syrian, racially, according to the Bible (Deuteronomy 26:5).

However, God made a covenant with Abraham which was postulated on grace. Abraham was saved by faith, as is every other lost sinner who receives salvation. Believers are, in this sense, called "children of Abraham." Christ is related on the human side to every great family division of the family of men. God came very close to us in the person of Christ. He could not have come any closer if he had chosen to become our personal brother in our immediate family.

The writer, in the fifth chapter of Hebrews, presents two qualifications for a priest. He shows that Christ met both of these requirements, in order to become the Great High Priest. First, the priest must be taken from among men. He must be related to man so that he might have a kindred feeling. He must be a man, for the priest represented man before God, and he must "have compassion on the ignorant, and on them that are out of the way; for that he himself is compassed with infirmity" (Hebrews 5:2). Secondly, the priest must be divinely appointed. Christ likewise meets this requirement, as the writer demonstrates with an abundance of quotations from other Scripture. We need not dwell on the second, as it has no direct bearing upon our subject; but the first bears on the kinship of Christ to the race of man. The writer to the Hebrews offers the kinship of Christ to the race as a proof of his priesthood. "The word was made flesh" is the simple yet sublime statement of John. It tells of the mighty passage of Deity to humanity, from heaven's glory to earth's gloom. Paul expresses the idea of the redeemer being near of kin when he gives this comprehensive account of the kinsman-redeemer: "But when the fulness of the time was come, God sent forth his Son, made of a woman, made under the law, to redeem them that were under the law, that we might receive the adoption of sons" (Galatians 4:4,5).

There could be no real redemption if Christ had not become our kinsman after the flesh. Redemption would only be a theological theory, tending to support a deistic and materialistic philosophy of life. The fact of the kinship of the redeemer puts a heart into this doctrine of redemption and delivers it from the coldness of rationalism. The universe in which we live is theocentric. God is the great central person of the universe and all things are for his glory. It is unimportant what man thinks and does. God is the only one who matters. His pleasure, his glory, his plan and his thoughts make the difference. Everything else is secondary. Modernism, in revolting from this seemingly cold position, made the universe Christocentric. This offered no final solution to the problem, for these split into two schools of thought. The deists at first held sway and robbed Christ of his deity, making him a philanthropic person. The pantheists then assumed control and they spoke of the divinity of Christ. The divinity which they contemplated was common to all men. At present the deists are becoming the more vigorous group.

There is a deliverance from the horns of this dilemma. The universe is theocentric, but it is not a formal affair. God became a man and came close to us for purposes of redemption. The universe is, also, as Henry Mabie put it, "redemptocentric." This enables man to retain his mental equilibrium in a universe suffering from the sting of sin. God did not leave man alone to beat his music out; but he came forth from heaven and became a man in order to redeem. He made himself kin to the man who had turned his back upon God. Man was marred by sin, but Christ became the perfect man. The man created in the Garden of Eden was made in the likeness of God. There was kinship in creation, for Adam is called "the son of God." Man alienated himself from the life of God, repudiated his right of kinship, and erased through spiritual death any likeness to God. God moved to restore the relationship, in a more permanent way, by coming down into flesh to redeem man from sin, and to recreate a more binding kinship where man might become the son of God through regeneration. It was "God in Christ, reconciling the world unto himself." Those who have been redeemed by Christ are in a position where now he "is not ashamed to call them brethren."

A mother is willing to sacrifice herself for the child of her bosom, because the little one is flesh of her flesh. A brother will fight for brother, even avenging any wrong done to him. Blood relationship begets in the heart an affection and love that is sometimes beyond human comprehension. There is an old bromide which recognizes this: "Blood is thicker than water." Human relationship is nothing in comparison with the love of God for lost sinners. He deliberately chose the place of kinship to us. His love not only compares with love of brother for brother but transcends it. Christ is the Kinsman-Redeemer of the world. "For God so loved the world, that he gave his only begotten Son."

We sinners have lost the right to claim any kinship to God; but God has restored a stronger tie through redemption. On the authority of God, we can claim to be sons of God if we are born again. There is one relationship that is not specifically granted to us to acknowledge, and that is to call Christ "our elder brother." Even James and Jude, who could have boasted of such a relationship, are satisfied to call themselves "servants of Jesus Christ." Certainly we are forbidden such liberty. But He is not ashamed to call us *brethren*.

CHAPTER 12

Redeemed Willingly

"Looking unto Jesus the author and finisher of our faith; who for the joy that was set before him endured the cross, despising the shame, and is set down at the right hand of the throne of God" (Hebrews 12:2).

The impressive feature about the story of Ruth and Boaz, which was emphasized in previous chapters, is the eagerness with which Boaz responded to the responsibility of a redeemer, and his glad assumption of that role. Most evidently he was intent upon paying whatever price was necessary, and in this he was in direct contrast to the "barefoot" kinsman. The other kinsman never exerted any initiative in the matter of redemption. Not until Boaz had called it to his attention did he express any willingness at all to redeem, and then he relinquished all his rights when he discovered that his inheritance would be endangered by his act of redemption. "And the kinsman said, I cannot redeem it for myself, lest I mar mine own inheritance: redeem thou my right to thyself; for I cannot redeem it" (Ruth 4:6).

There was no compulsion placed on the redeemer by the Mosaic statute. He could of his own volition act as a *goel*, or he could desist from exercising any rights that accrued to him under this law. The language of the law is specific: "After that he is sold he *may* be redeemed again; one of his brethren *may* redeem him" (Leviticus 25:48). The only constraint was the blood tie. If love for his more unfortunate brother did not prompt him to act, then there was no law which could force him to do so. The "barefoot" kinsman's interest in Ruth and Naomi was nil; and he was not legally bound to act, though a moral obligation might rest upon him. Seemingly, nothing moved him, and there was no power to make him move.

This is the first point of difference between Boaz and the other kinsman. There was a willingness on the part of Boaz. The urgency of the man, in the whole matter, is patently evident. The source of his inspiration does not have to be sought afar. When Naomi and Ruth returned from the land of Moab, Boaz was apparently not one of the townsfolk to greet them. He did not know who Ruth was when she came into his field, though he had heard of her. Jamieson, Fausset and Brown offer the explanation that Boaz was away upon some military expedition at the time of their homecoming. The first information that Boaz had concerning the return of Naomi was a report that contained a favorable and complimentary estimate of the stranger who had come with her: "And Boaz answered and said unto her, It hath fully been showed me, all that thou hast done unto thy mother-in-law since the death of thine husband: and how thou hast left thy father and thy mother, and the land of thy nativity, and art come unto a people which thou knewest not heretofore" (Ruth 2:11).

The return of Naomi, and the presence of a delightful stranger, did not prompt Boaz to go immediately to the aid of his distressed kinsfolk. An apology may be found for Boaz in the probability that not enough time had elapsed between their return and his meeting with Ruth to enable him to do anything tangible.

It was the meeting of Boaz with Ruth in the field which led the *goel* to act and to set the wheels of redemption in motion. The inquiry that he made of his servant in charge of the reapers is significant: "Whose damsel is this?" His evident interest in Ruth, from the moment of meeting, must have been apparent to all and certainly it did not escape the attention of Ruth. Her question to him was surely guileless and artless, but it revealed an undue attention on his part: "Then she fell on her face, and bowed herself to the ground, and said unto him, Why have I found grace in thine eyes, that thou shouldest take knowledge of me, seeing I am a stranger?" (Ruth 2:10). Boaz insisted that Ruth continue to glean in his fields so that he might make adequate provision for her. The first day's gleaning was so much that Naomi did not let it go unnoticed, but was provoked to inquire, "Where hast thou gleaned today?" Naomi could see, with her mother's heart of experience, all the evidence of a man who had fallen desperately in love with a woman. Nothing but love could have led to the manifestation of such grace. The name Ruth may not sustain the meaning of "beauty" that is sometimes given to it, but most assuredly the story of this book would lead us to ascribe that characteristic to the one who bore it. The Moabitess stirred the heart of Boaz. John Lord makes Heloise, loved by Abelard, the symbol of love among women. In our feeble judgment, Ruth surpasses Heloise as a fitting symbol of the noblest passion among mankind. Ruth of the Bible transcends Heloise of secular history as a living example of what is finest in human affection.

Naomi, recognizing the implications, was bold enough to suggest that Boaz was in love with her pretty daughter-in-law. "Then Naomi her mother in law said unto her, My daughter, shall I not seek rest for thee, that it may be well with thee?" (Ruth 3:1). The "rest" to which Naomi referred was that of a home for her widowed daughter-in-law. "It was a home to which Naomi pointed, a home for her daughter's heart."

That it was the intention of Boaz to marry Ruth was the accurate assumption of Naomi, and the story of chapter three is predicated upon that supposition. The Authorized Version does not bring out that idea sharply, but Gesenius' translation of

134

Ruth 3:13 makes it clear. "If he will marry thee by right of relationship, let him marry thee, but if he will not, I will marry thee."

Gesenius gives a fourth meaning for the Hebrew word *goel*, which was known by those in the Book of Ruth and which was acted upon by them. According to the law of Moses, when a man died, it was the office of the next of kin to marry his widow (Deuteronomy 25:5-10). When Ruth went to the threshing floor of Boaz, she was not breaking through the bounds of modesty and propriety. She was entirely within the moral code of Israel. She was following it to the very letter, and according to the instructions of Naomi. It is evident from Gesenius' translation in the preceding passage that Boaz recognized this obligation under the Mosaic code; and it may be said to his credit that he had no intention of transgressing the Mosaic law at this point. The language of Boaz corresponds to our present-day proposal of marriage, although it is couched in a form to comply with the law and custom of that day. Naomi so interpreted his language and action, as she intimated in her admonition to Ruth: "Then said she, Sit still, my daughter, until thou know how the matter will fall: for the man will not be in rest, until he have finished the thing this day" (Ruth 3:18).

The fourth chapter of Ruth outlines the action of Boaz on behalf of the stranger. He immediately started the legal wheels moving. He haled the other kinsman into court and laid upon him the necessity of action in regard to the parcel of ground of Elimelech. The other kinsman was perfectly willing to redeem the land until Boaz revealed to him that there was more involved than the property. Besides the ground, there was the girl. She was the one who moved Boaz to action, and she was the one who prompted the anonymous kinsman to desist. The unknown kinsman relinquished all his claims, and immediately Boaz seized them; and a contract was made then and there which conveyed to Boaz, the party of the second part, all rights as redeemer appertaining to the estate of Elimelech.

Boaz was more than willing to become the redeemer; he was eager to function in that capacity. He acted with enthusiasm in that relationship. The motive which prompted him to action was love for the Moabitess. Although a stranger, she possessed beauty, and withal a charm and character which had rightly earned for her a worthy name in the land of her adoption. Her excellent treatment of her mother-in-law and her sincere passion for her must have moved the citizens of Bethlehem in that day; and even today she stands out as one of the loveliest characters in the Bible. Willingness is a feeble word to describe the attitude of Boaz in the role of a kinsman-redeemer. *Eagerness* is a more appropriate term.

Christ who is greater than Boaz had his volition fully committed to the task of the great kinsman-redeemer of the human family. Christ was in no way an unwilling redeemer, nor was he forced into that position by circumstances over which he had no control. He defined his own attitude toward the cross: "No man taketh it [life] from me, but I lay it down of myself. I have power to lay it down, and I have power to take it again" (John 10:18). The cross was not something he sought to avoid, but he "for the joy that was set before him endured the cross" (Hebrews 12:2). Again he said, in reference to his death: "Even as the Son of man came not to be ministered unto, but to minister, and to give his life a ransom for many" (Matthew 20:28).

There are two extreme positions regarding the death of Christ that need to be avoided. To avoid shipwreck it is necessary to steer the craft of one's thinking between this Scylla and Charybdis. While we attempt to avoid one extreme, there is always present the danger of falling into the other. The first extreme is the assumption that Christ was forced to die on the cross. This is a grievous error. Christ was not compelled to die on the cross by outside forces which he could not control; otherwise, God would have been guilty of murder, for "it pleased the Lord to bruise him; he hath put him to grief." Christ was a *willing* sacrifice. He was obedient unto death, it is true, but it was an obedience that had gained the permission of his volition.

The other extreme is the supposition that the death of Christ was a suicide. This, too, is a glaring falsehood. His willingness to die was not born of a desire to leave off living. He did not love death but dreaded it as such, a fact which the experience in the Garden of Gethsemane indicates. A mother who plunges into the flames of a burning house to rescue her baby, knowing full well that the holocaust will be her deathbed, is not a suicide. She goes willingly and gladly because her child must be rescued from the flames, and this woman, with such a motive, is praised as a martyr. If she deliberately chooses death, merely for the sake of dying, then she is a poor miserable wretch of a suicide. Again, if she is pushed into the fire against her will, the hand that pushed her belongs to a murderer. But when she willingly enters the fiery furnace, the moral problem is removed, and she is acclaimed as a heroine.

Isaiah, the prophet who more clearly than any other depicted the death of Christ, declared, "He was oppressed, and he was afflicted, yet he opened not his mouth" (Isaiah 53:7). The gospel affirms this statement in a striking manner. Christ did not protest at his own trial. It was evident that he was not trying to escape the penalty which his enemies sought to inflict upon him. Calmly, he faced the issue, accepted the verdict, made no appeal for help, bore in silence the unjust penalty imposed upon him, and died as "the Lamb of God, which taketh away the sin of the world." All this was in fulfillment of the Old Testament declaration: "As a sheep before her shearers is dumb, so he openeth not his mouth." Paul appealed to Caesar for justice, but Christ made no appeal from an unjust sentence to a higher authority, for the sinner deserved to die and Christ was bearing the penalty of sin willingly.

His life was the ransom for many. That is the scriptural explanation for the death of Christ, coming from his own lips before the excitement of the last few days of his earthly life. His passivity in the hands of his captors would be tantamount to suicide if it were not for the fact that he was dying for another. He was a kinsman-redeemer, paying the price of redemption. The only poised position which can be maintained regarding the death of Christ is to see him as *the* Kinsman-Redeemer, performing the work of redemption willingly. He deliberately drank the cup. With eagerness he endured the cross, and with joyful anticipation he accepted his passion. Tears of joy were mingled with his tears of suffering. He willingly bore your sin and paid the price for your redemption. He not only endangered his inheritance but he sacrificed his life. Love made him willing to die, for he "first loved us." He did not find the motive for redemption in us, but he found it in his own person. We were not lovely, but he was wonderful. He redeemed us because of his yearning love. Now we can say exultantly with Paul: "I live by the faith of the Son of God, who loved me, and gave himself for me" (Galatians 2:20).

CHAPTER 13

No Risk Too Great

Regardless of the translation placed upon the first verse of chapter two, where Boaz is called "a mighty man of wealth," the evident implication is that he was thoroughly capable of performing the part of kinsman-redeemer per se. There is not a scintilla of suggestion that Boaz was unable to render the adequate service of a kinsman-redeemer. Rather the tenor of the story suggests that he was more than able to redeem. As a man of wealth, he could pay the price; as a man of valor, he possessed the strength necessary to enforce his claim; and as a man of the law, he was fully prepared to fulfill all legal requirements.

The presence of another redeemer with prior claims *de jure* was the only obstacle that seemed to preclude the possibility of Boaz' acting the kinsman's part. The anonymous kinsman presents to us the major problem of the story of Ruth. The story recognizes that he was the kinsman nearer than Boaz. Not only did he lack a willingness to redeem, but he lacked the ability to redeem. The problem resolves itself upon the ability of the two redeemers. Both of them were in the unique position of kinsmen-redeemers, with the unnamed kinsman possessing the advantage in that he was nearer of kin than Boaz. Yet, in the final analysis, this kinsman confessed that he could not redeem without affecting his own inheritance. At the same time he stated that Boaz occupied no such anomalous position. He urged Boaz to redeem.

Now, what made the difference between these two redeemers so that one had difficulties which prevented him from acting, while the other had these difficulties obviated? There is nothing in the story that offers any explanation, while in the Mosaic system there is nothing forthcoming that throws any light upon this moot problem. This is a difficulty largely ignored by commentators, for the sufficient reason that there is no explanation. We raise the question, not to answer it, but to recognize it. The recognition of this problem furnishes an understanding of the kinsman-redeemer. The redeemer had to be a kinsman and had to be willing, but he might meet these two requirements and still be wholly inadequate because of inability. The "barefoot" kinsman possessed the first two essentials. Boaz possessed an ability that the unnamed kinsman lacked. It was something besides a willingness, for this kinsman did not refuse to redeem but expressed his willingness when the matter was called to his attention. "I will redeem it." The kinsman went on to declare that there was a difference between himself and Boaz. Although he was closer of kin and possessed all claims of priority, Boaz could redeem without incurring the liability which was placed upon him. The presence of the Moabitess, and her rights to the property, indicated that it would be difficult for an Israelite to get a clear title to the property. It is quite probable that this other kinsman had a wife and children, and if he redeemed the property in which Ruth had an inheritance, it would in all probability affect his family estate which would be inherited by his children.

Boaz was unmarried, and there was no such difficulty for him. When he married the Moabitess, he brought her into the congregation of the Lord by giving her his name and all the rights appertaining thereto. This is merely conjecture and is not offered as the interpretation of the story, but is offered to demonstrate a reasonable and probable explanation of the difficulty.

Although it is difficult to offer a solution to this problem, it is not impossible. The Mosaic law did not treat this matter. The Mosaic system dealt with great legal principles and with the most important issues touching life, but it did not offer detailed laws touching every relationship of life.

For example, the sixth commandment said, "Thou shalt not kill" (Exodus 20:13). The penalty for committing murder was also given, but none of the details were given as to how to determine what constituted murder, and no distinction between manslaughter and murder was given. It was evident, however, that they made some such distinction, as is seen in the law concerning the cities of refuge (Numbers 35:1-34; Deuteronomy 19:1-6). Custom must have established some sort of precedent which had the sanction of God.

Boaz possessed the power to redeem and he exercised his power on behalf of Ruth. The law kept her out (Deuteronomy 23:3), but Boaz used his ability as a redeemer to redeem her from the power of the law. She was a stranger, far removed from the privileges granted to God's people, and unable to extricate herself from the meshes of the law; but a mighty man of wealth paid the price and brought her into the nation, into his home and into his heart. This absorbing and captivating story of redeeming love was but a faint adumbration of Christ who was mightier than Boaz and who paid a far greater price.

The highest title borne by Jesus Christ is that of redeemer. It is far greater than that of Rabbi, Lord, Master, or King of kings and Lord of lords. As a teacher, he was the greatest that the world has ever seen. Even the enemies of the cross have been unanimous down through the ages in asserting that he was *the* great teacher. He set an example that has been unparalleled in the annals of history. His life has been the subject of admiration by even the skeptic. Renan, the great French agnostic, admired the life of Christ, for he makes that the subject of his greatest work. Yet, as example and teacher, Christ does not possess his highest title. These titles are not to be ignored or taken from him, but it is in the title of *redeemer* that all the others receive life and meaning. Frederick A. Noble has expressed it in this language: "It is not to be denied that Christ is much other to us than a redeemer . . . In the first place, both his instruction and his example miss their highest value without the large and crowning benefit which comes from his death. For grant, what has just been claimed, that in his words He plucks and brings to us the flower of knowledge, that in his perfect demeanor, in the midst of friends and foes alike, under favoring circumstances and also under perplexities and temptations and trials, He illustrates for us the ideal of daily conduct; yet of what service would it all be to us without atoning blood to wash away the defilements that are in us, and to emancipate our souls from the dominance of sin? If knowledge is to be of advantage to one, he must be in condition to use knowledge. If a perfect example is to be of worth, one must somehow be possessed of ability to imitate the example."

The title of redeemer enhances the meaning of the others. It is one of the prophetic titles given to Christ in the Old Testament. It was first given to him by Job through prophetic inspiration. "For I know that my redeemer liveth, and that he shall stand at the latter day upon the earth" (Job 19:25). This comes from what is probably the oldest book in the Bible, and expresses the heart cry of man from ancient days. The prophet looked down the vista of time to the end of man's sorry attempt to rule this earth, and saw the Saviour in the last days bearing this high title: "And the Redeemer shall come to Zion" (Isaiah 59:20). Israel, in view of this and similar prophecies, anticipated the coming of a redeemer. Jehovah came to be in every sense their Redeemer. The coming Redeemer could be none other than Jehovah; although these two ideas were never merged into one definite statement, it was, nevertheless, the heart hope of Israel.

It is well to observe that nowhere in the New Testament is Christ given the title of redeemer, but he was given a name which bore all the significance of the appellation. The anouncement of the angel Gabriel to Mary revealed that name. It was the name *Joshua* which in the Greek is *Jesus*. Simply stated, it meant "the salvation of Jehovah," or "Jehovah is a Saviour." The name was not spoken the first time by Gabriel. Joshua, the man who succeeded Moses, was the first to bear this name with distinction, and after him there must have been many boys who bore that name. At the time of our Lord's birth, there must have been a great company of boys bearing that name. Every Hebrew mother anticipated that the son born to her would be the deliverer. It was only in Jesus Christ, however, that the name found adequate fulfillment. The angel announced to Joseph that the name signified that Jesus would "save his people from their sins" (Matthew 1:21). Redemption became the subject of the spiritual songs of prophecy uttered at his birth, first by Zacharias (Luke 1:68), and then by Anna (Luke 2:38.)

Jesus bore that name in the unique way of redeemer, and he alone so adorns it that it might find its final fruition. The name Jesus is reserved for only one today. That name belongs supremely to the one who hung on the cross. It was the name Jesus which was written above the impaled figure. This is the name that he brought out of the tomb and glorified. Paul, in speaking of his transition from heaven to earth and the humiliation that such a movement entailed, also told of his passage back to heaven and the exaltation that such a movement involved. The round trip that he made from heaven to earth accomplished the work of redemption. He is today something that he could not have been before he came to this earth. He is a redeemer today by virtue of the work accomplished on the cross. He received a name which he would not otherwise bear if he had not come to this earth. It was the name of Jesus. He came down to this place of humiliation to receive that name, in order that he might bear it back and exalt it as the greatest name ever borne by man. Paul told of the conspicuous place that name occupied and will continue to occupy in God's program. "Wherefore God also hath highly exalted him, and given him a name which is above every name: that at the name of Jesus every knee should bow, of things in heaven, and things in earth, and things under the earth; and that every tongue should confess that Jesus Christ is Lord, to the glory of God the Father" (Philippians 2:9-11).

It is as the Redeemer that Christ received the name of Jesus. That human name implied all that the term kinsman-redeemer could imply.

There was another implication in the name of

Jesus which emphasized his deity as well as his humanity. The name meant that Jehovah was the Saviour. It was God who became a man, and that man bore the name of Jesus. The Gospel of John, which sets forth his deity, uses the name of Jesus almost exclusively. His human name occurs more than any other, which suggests that God became the man, Jesus, or as Jesus expressed it in this Gospel, "I came forth from the Father, and am come into the world: again, I leave the world, and go to the Father" (John 16:28).

Jesus is mightier than Boaz because he is able to redeem lost sinners. He is able because he was God manifest in human flesh, and he can do all that God can do. He brought to bear on the work of redemption all the wisdom and power of God. Jesus was the omnipotent Redeemer. We will now consider two passages of Scripture which set forth Jesus as the Redeemer who has the ability to redeem.

The first passage is an extended one and we shall forbear quoting it, as there are only portions of it that we wish to examine. The entire passage is John 10:11-30, but the verses that bear on our subject are verses 11,14-18,27-30. In this section of Scripture, under the figure of a shepherd, our Lord is set forth as the Redeemer who has the ability to redeem. He is the Good Shepherd who gives his life for the sheep. Three times over he emphasizes the fact that the Shepherd will die for the sheep (verses 11, 15, 17). He also emphasizes the fact that his death for the sheep will not only be a willing death but a death over which he has the power. He had the power to lay his life down and he had power to take it up again. His work of redemption is wrought in the power of deity.

These sheep, whom he redeems by his death, are the objects of eternal life vouchsafed to them by his death. Not only is the Redeemer omnipotent, not only is his redemption wrought in the power of deity, but the redemption itself is a mighty redemption. "They shall never perish" speaks of the new position into which the sheep are brought. The explanation for that is found in the power of the Redeemer, "neither shall any man pluck them out of my hand" (verse 28). Then, as if that were not enough, our Lord tells of another hand, the hand of the Father which is clasped over them for eternal security. He appears to be saying that he holds them in the left hand of deity, and that the Father clasps the right hand of deity over them. The omnipotent Redeemer holds the redeemed. The final perseverance of the saints is possible on the basis of the holding power of God.

This passage reveals the limit to which God is going to redeem lost sinners. It is an infinite extent that appears to be extravagant, and a price that seems to be exorbitant, but the Good Shepherd is "a mighty man of wealth." The justification for this exceedingly lavish expenditure is found in the place to which the sinners are redeemed, even "eternal life."

The second passage, which reveals the ability of our Redeemer, is found in the Epistle to the Hebrews. "Wherefore he is able also to save them to the uttermost that come unto God by him, seeing he ever liveth to make intercession for them" (Hebrews 7:25). It is the interpretation of some commentators that the reference here is not to the depths of sin out of which the sinner is saved, but rather to the other extreme of redemption, the consummation after it is once initiated. Jamieson, Fausset and Brown give "altogether" and "perfectly" as an interpretation of the expression "to the uttermost." This is the interpretation that is concurred with here, but this does not preclude the other position that the reference is likewise to the depths to which the Redeemer went to save lost sinners. Kelly interprets it as "the guarantee of a commensurate salvation." Delitzsch sees in this expression no reference to time, but of every want and need met in Christ.

Regardless of which phase of redemption is considered—the place from which the Redeemer takes the sinner or the place to which the Redeemer brings the sinner—something of the great power expended in redemption is the evident intention of the writer here. "To the uttermost" implies *from* the uttermost. This is an a priori consideration, for redemption finds its cause in the lost estate of the sinner, and its effect in eternal life. No matter how far down Jesus goes to get the sinner, he is able to bring him all the way to the consummation of redemption. Scofield suggests, in a footnote, "completely" as a meaning for the expression "to the uttermost." This again logically suggests that redemption is a process. The sinner is lost, "having no hope, and without God in the world." God lifts his mighty arm in redemption, and begins to move on behalf of the sinner, and, lo! the lost sinners, "who sometimes were far off are made nigh by the blood of Christ." For the sinner, this may only consume a moment of time, as this is not a chronological process. It is a process which begins with the sinner absolutely lost and which leaves him absolutely saved. The sinner passes from death unto life; and it takes a long bridge, and a mighty one, to span the yawning chasm between these two extremes.

"Our Boaz" found us "aliens from the commonwealth of Israel," and with sin preventing us from ever entering the congregation of the Lord. However, there was another kinsman who had an opportunity to redeem sinners. There is another way of salvation, theoretically. There is a hypothesis on which to erect a plan of salvation. Dr. Grant calls attention to this assumed redeemer. This hypothetical plan of salvation is stated in Scripture: "Again, when the wicked man turneth away from his wickedness that he hath committed, and doeth that which is lawful and right, he shall save his soul alive" (Ezekiel 18:27). This is a plan of salvation for a wicked man whereby he can become his own redeemer. God put Israel on the same sort of basis at Sinai. "Now therefore, if ye will obey my voice indeed, and keep my covenant, then ye shall be a peculiar treasure unto me above all people: for all the earth is mine" (Exodus 19:5). This is the salvation by works. The law becomes the redeemer in this plan of salvation. In fifteen hundred years of Israel's history, it was obviously proven that this plan would not save a soul. It is evident that not one soul in Israel was saved by the law. This was a plan of self-recovery, given to Israel to see if man could redeem himself by law. The law became the despair of Israel, and finally became their undoing. Law is the kinsman who is even closer to man, just as the other kinsman was closer than Boaz. But in the final analysis, the law could not redeem man without endangering its own inheritance, which was its high standard.

Law today, as such, cannot redeem man without lowering its standards to conform to man's weak ability. If it did come down to the low plane where man could abide by its precepts, it would no longer be law, but would be a system of compromise with a very low standard. God would have a law to pardon sinners which would not change the sinner except to fill him with blind pride in the idea that his sin was well-pleasing to God. Law demands a high standard to conform to the character of God. This high plane is above man and condemns man. "For as many as are of the works of the law are under the curse: for it is written, Cursed is every one that continueth not in all things which are written in the book of the law to do them" (Galatians 3:10).

Salvation by works is a plan of redemption, but it is like the anonymous kinsman who had to retire on behalf of Boaz. Salvation by works cannot save a lost soul, for "by the deeds of the law there shall no flesh be justified in his sight: for by the law is the knowledge of sin" (Romans 3:20). Naomi and Ruth would have been permanently undone if they had placed any faith in the "barefoot" kinsman, for he was impotent to redeem them. It was only in Boaz that they found complete redemption. Salvation by

151

works cannot save a lost soul; and it is tragic to trust such a redeemer. Salvation by faith in Christ Jesus is the only plan that finally works. "Knowing that a man is not justified by the works of the law, but by the faith of Jesus Christ, even we have believed in Jesus Christ, that we might be justified by the faith of Christ, and not by the works of the law: for by the works of the law shall no flesh be justified" (Galatians 2:16). Faith in our Kinsman-Redeemer is the only plan of salvation which is effective for we have a Kinsman-Redeemer who is able to save the last, the least and the lost.

CHAPTER 14

Not for Himself

The redeemer must not only be a kinsman; but he must belong to a higher branch of the family, where he is not involved in the trouble of the family. The redeemer must not be under the curse which makes redemption essential for another. If an Israelite was himself in slavery because of untoward circumstances or misfortune, he could not act as a redeemer. Rather, he himself needed a redeemer.

Boaz, for example, could not have acted in the capacity of redeemer if he had sold himself into slavery, or if he had been a Moabite. The demands of the law could not go unfulfilled in him, nor could the curse of exclusion by the law, because of some defect in his life, go unnoticed when he made application as a redeemer. A drowning man is in no position to rescue someone else who is drowning. A man who rescues people who are in a sinking ship cannot himself be in that sinking ship. The lifeline must be thrown by someone who is in a place of comparative safety. For someone to throw a lifeline from the upper deck of a sinking ship to someone on a lower deck will avail nothing.

The Chaldean translation of this moot phrase in verse one of chapter two is significant at this juncture. Boaz is called therein "a mighty man of law." Before the law, Boaz was a mighty man. This could mean the same thing that Paul intended when he wrote, "Touching the righteousness which is in the law, blameless" (Philippians 3:6). Boaz had met every demand of the law concerning offerings for sin. He had made all proper sacrifices. He had met every demand of the Mosaic law, and it had no claim upon him which would prevent his acting as redeemer.

Not only did he meet the law in his conduct but he met its just demands in his character. The genealogy in Ruth was David's genealogy, which linked him with the tribe of Judah. This same genealogy was Christ's, which gave the Lord the legal right to the throne of David. This genealogy belonged to Boaz also, and it conveyed to him all that was conveyed to David and Christ. He was in the chosen line. He was an Israelite, and the prerogatives of the nation belonged to him. "Who are Israelites; to whom pertaineth the adoption, and the glory, and the covenants, and the giving of the law, and the service of God, and the promises; whose are the fathers, and of whom as concerning

154

the flesh Christ came, who is over all, God blessed for ever. Amen" (Romans 9:4,5). There could be no objection to Boaz, racially, as a redeemer.

Boaz was a rich man. The implication is that he had never been forced to sell himself into slavery or to dispose of his property, even temporarily. As a slave he would have been under the curse, which would have incapacitated him to act as redeemer and would have put him in need of a deliverer. His hands were not shackled by slavery. He was free to act from the outside on behalf of the poor kinsman who needed redemption.

Christ fully met this requirement of a redeemer. He was free from the curse of sin. He was not vulnerable at any point to its deadening effects. "Hereafter I will not talk much with you: for the prince of this world cometh, and hath nothing in me" (John 14:30). The law was not given to silence him, for he did not break it but kept it in all its points. "Think not that I am come to destroy the law, or the prophets: I am not come to destroy, but to fulfil" (Matthew 5:17).

He was not a Gentile who never attempted to keep its precepts, but he was "made under the law" (Galatians 4:4). He kept it in all of its parts.

Christ was unique inasmuch as it could not be said of the other children of men, not even Adam, that they were "holy, harmless, undefiled, separate from sinners" (Hebrews 7:26). Before he was born the angel Gabriel said to his mother, "That holy thing which shall be born of thee shall be called the Son of God" (Luke 1:35). Mary had the most wonderful child in the world. There never was one like him before, and there never has been one since. The first child born into the world inherited the fallen nature from his parents. His mother, Eve, thought he might be the one to bruise the serpent's head, and so she called him Cain, for she said, "I have gotten a [the] man from the Lord." However, this child was not a redeemer but was the first murderer. All children from that day on have manifested the propensities of sin. That has been the indelible mark on the sons of Adam.

The one exception to the rule is Jesus Christ. He possessed no inherent sin. He had no sinful nature. He was virgin born. In his lifetime he challenged anyone to convict him of sin, which challenge was never accepted or claim successfully refuted. He was the sinless Saviour. He was the impeccable Christ. As the only sinless person, he was not subject to death as the race of man is. He testified that he would "give his life a ransom for many." He was outside the power of death, but he moved under its power that he might become the redeemer. "And deliver them who through fear of death were all their lifetime subject to bondage" (Hebrews 2:15). The Son of God was free to redeem, because he was not implicated in man's sin in any way. When he went to the cross, our sin became his, and he "was made sin for us who knew no sin."

Christ was not only the Kinsman-Redeemer, but, racially, he was an Israelite. He was the son of Abraham, Isaac and Jacob. He was descended from the line of David. His mother was a daughter of Israel. He must have resembled members of that race, for the woman at the well in Samaria asked him, "How is it that thou, being a Jew, askest drink of me, which am a woman of Samaria?" Although he was free from the sinful nature that belongs to the sons of Adam, he was not a stranger but was identified with the covenant people and the chosen nation. He was not outside the human family because of his sinless nature.

Jesus Christ presented all the credentials of a kinsman-redeemer when he came to this earth. He was not like Moses who attempted to deliver his brethren in Egypt without any instructions from God. Christ was not born under the slavery of sin. He was able to pay the penalty of sin because he was not himself subject to it. When he throws the lifeline to some sinking soul, he is able to rescue, for he stands upon the vantage ground of a sinless life. When he went to the cross, he was not paying any penalty for himself. He was absolutely absolved from the curse and penalty of sin. It was the slavery and the sin of *man* that he was bearing on the cross.

CHAPTER 15

No Price Too High

"Forasmuch as ye know that ye were not redeemed with corruptible things, as silver and gold, from your vain conversation received by tradition from your fathers; but with the precious blood of Christ, as of a lamb without blemish and without spot" (I Peter 1:18,19).

The kinsman-redeemer must have the legal tender of redemption. In other words, the redeemer must have the price which is the legal amount essential to make the deliverance. He must be able to discharge the obligation fully. In the case of Boaz this must have been a small matter. It was no difficulty for Boaz, the rich kinsman, to redeem the small estate of Elimelech. In the text the question of the amount is never raised, nor is it discussed as a probable hindrance toward making redemption. Even the other kinsman was willing, and therefore was apparently able to pay the amount that was required to free the property. In this matter he was unlike Christ, for the price paid by Christ for our redemption was tremendous and bankrupted heaven temporarily. It drained all the resources of an omnipotent God. Christ could pay and he did pay, but at what a cost! "For ye know the grace of our Lord Jesus Christ, that, though he was rich, yet for your sakes he became poor, that ye through his poverty might be rich" (II Corinthians 8:9).

1. *The Redeemer Must Have the Redemptive Price.*
It is necessary to ascertain the legal tender Christ used in accomplishing redemption for man. It will be necessary to return, for the moment, to the redemption of Israel out of Egypt. The night of the Passover marked the time of the accomplishment of Israel's redemption. That night was the birthday of the nation. They were born at night in the brickyards of Egypt. God told them that it would be "the beginning of months" for them. They were instructed to take a lamb for each house and to slay it. The blood of the lamb was taken and sprinkled on the doorposts and lintels of the homes of the Hebrews that evening. The death angel visited every home in Egypt that night; and at each home where he found the blood sprinkled, he passed over. But where the blood was not sprinkled, death seized upon the firstborn of that family, both man and beast. The sign of the Passover was blood. The nation of Israel began on a bloody basis. They were

redeemed that first Passover night by blood.

Why was the blood brought into this great prominence? It could never be a beautiful thing to see. The sight of blood produces a sort of nausea in most people. It is repulsive to the thought of man. The blood could not have been chosen because of its appeal to the aesthetic nature of man. Blood repels because it is abhorred by the normal person. Redemption by blood has been abhorred by the natural man from the time that Cain brought the lovely fruit of the cursed ground as a sacrifice for his sin up to the bold modernism of the present hour. The hideous specter of a bloody lamb offended Cain's nobler feelings, but in reality it was his fallen nature rebelling against God's way. Dr. Coffin quotes from a poem of an unnamed poetess to give expression to the modern reaction to the blood of Christ.

"Go, bitter Christ, grim Christ! haul if Thou wilt
Thy bloody cross to Thine own bleak Calvary!
When did I bid Thee suffer for my guilt
To bind intolerable claims on me?
I loathe Thy sacrifice; I am sick of Thee."

Certainly God was not seeking to emphasize beauty in religion, nor was he attempting to please the natural man when he instituted the bloody sacrifice. The explanation was contained in the Levitical ritual: "For the life of the flesh is in the blood: and I have given it to you upon the altar to make an atonement for your souls: for it is the blood that maketh an atonement for the soul" (Leviticus 17:11).

The blood is the life principle of man. The blood represents the life. The shedding of the blood of animals sets forth the sacrificing of life in substitution for the one making the sacrifice. But why should it be necessary for man to have a substitute to shed blood for him? Why was man's life demanded? The human race stood in disobedience to the will of God, in rebellion to the authority of God, in treason to the government of God, and in ingratitude to the love of God. The simple but satisfactory statement of Scripture is: "All have sinned, and come short of the glory of God." Man is a sinner in any way you care to look at him. Before God, man is guilty. There must be some penalty for a sinner, or else God is not the moral ruler of this universe. There is such a penalty, for there comes thundering down from the throne of justice, out of the presence of a holy God, the eternal and irrevocable law: "The soul that sinneth, it shall die." This places every man under the sentence of death, for "the wages of sin is death." The sons of Adam have faithfully drawn wages for the penalty of sin, as every cemetery silently testifies. Physical death is the outward evidence of the accuracy of this law. Physical death is not all, for spiritual death is included, which death means eternal separation from God.

The only hope for man is to get someone to pay a penalty for him which is satisfactory to God. It is reasonable that the death of animals could not atone for sins. "For it is not possible that the blood of bulls and of goats should take away sins" (Hebrews 10:4). There must be found some man, who is

161

satisfactory to God, who is willing to pay with his blood the price of redemption for the penalty of sin. The big problem is to find someone satisfactory to God. We have noted that he must be related to the human family by blood; but if he has the blood of Adam flowing through his veins, he, too, will need a substitute. It is impossible for man to produce a redeemer who can pay the price of redemption. No man can be free from the guilt of sin, and no man can escape its penalty for himself. As far as man is concerned, redemption is an impossible achievement. No man can present anything that will be legal tender in heaven; no man can even redeem himself. In his own strength, man is hopelessly lost for eternity.

It is at this juncture that God steps into the picture with a price that was legal tender in heaven. God issued the currency that redeemed man. That story is told in this sublime language: "Wherefore when he cometh into the world, he saith, Sacrifice and offering thou wouldest not, but a body hast thou prepared me" (Hebrews 10:5).

The blood of bulls and goats could not redeem man. The blood of man could not redeem man. So God took upon himself a human body. This body was not contaminated with the sin nature. No tainted blood flowed through his body. This blood, which was free from sin, was the source of his earthly life. He shed this blood, and thereby sacrificed the life of this earthly body for the payment in full of man's redemption. Twenty-one times Scripture identifies the blood of the Lord Jesus Christ as the legal tender of redemption.

The value of any currency is measured in what it can accomplish. Currency is worthless when it is not acceptable for articles of value. Currency is valuable when it is accepted for things of value. What is the purchasing power of money? This is the only worthwhile question regarding it. Some express their philosophy in this way: "I am not interested in money as such, but in what money can buy." This test may be applied to the blood of Christ. Putnam mentions ten wonderful and priceless objectives made possible by the blood of Christ. Wilkes enumerates fourteen marvelous accomplishments made available to man by the blood of Christ. Each one of these is a spiritual blessing that cannot be measured in terms of dollars and cents. Nothing in this world can buy any one of them. We do not wish to deal with these items; but we do wish to mention just one blessing that has been bought by the blood of Christ, and which has been omitted by all works on redemption consulted for this thesis.

2. *The Privileges of Heaven Have Been Purchased for Lost Sinners by the Blood of Christ.*

"And they sang a new song, saying, Thou art worthy to take the book, and to open the seals thereof: for thou wast slain, and hast redeemed us to God by thy blood out of every kindred, and tongue, and people, and nation" (Revelation 5:9).

Every normal individual entertains a desire to go to heaven. Each one may have a very limited and faulty conception of heaven, and perhaps may be devoid of any spiritual appreciation of it; but he secretly cherishes a wish to go there someday. Even the worst sinner would like to go to heaven, even if it only meant to him the escape from punishment. Heaven is a place in the thinking of all peoples, whether they expect to go there or not; and to them it is a place of unspeakable pleasures and joys forevermore. The human race is characterized by a deep urge to gain heaven. As men approach death, the desire for heaven increases. Men on their deathbeds would give all they possess to be assured that they would go there. Any man who could assure the members of the human race that they would go to heaven on the payment of a stipulated sum to him would find himself the richest man on earth, able to gratify the avarice of any Midas.

In the final analysis, men will pay more for the chance of going to this cherished place than for any other thing. The millions of dollars paid into the coffers of the Roman Catholic Church annually to get some loved one out of purgatory is a witness to this innate yearning of the heart of man. What a ghastly and awful thing it is to traffic in human souls as if some human agency had divine authority over their place of abode after death! This fiction of purgatory has created the wealthiest organization on earth. Billions are spent annually by men for pleasure and security. As these two objectives are present in every conception of heaven, this money would be gladly diverted into the channel which would guarantee heaven to the natural man, apart from God's plan of salvation. Every man will invest money in a feasible human plan which will make heaven available to him.

In the ninth verse of the fifth chapter of Revelation, there is presented a company of people from every nook and corner of the earth. Every race, class and condition of man is present. This company is present in heaven. They are singing because of the fact that they have been brought into the blessings of this place—heaven. They do not attribute their presence there to anything that they have done, or to any price that they have been able to make in payment of this exceedingly great privilege. Yet, they acknowledge that someone did pay a price to make it possible for them to be there. The purchase price which made heaven available to them is not in the coin of earth, such as silver and gold. They are there on their own confession that they have been redeemed by the blood of the Lamb. The blood of Christ is the most valuable thing in this universe because it has purchased what silver and gold cannot; and yet men would be willing to sell all their possessions that they might buy heaven. Another sold all that he had and paid the price of their redemption.

There is another fact that gives value to any currency. This is the scarcity of it. Inflation destroys the value of any money. There has been only one person who ever lived who could "give his life a ransom for many." Only one person out of the millions of the earth, ever shed blood that availed before God. There have been literally millions of martyrs, but only the death of one redeemed sinners from the penalty of sin. The blood of Christ is today, and has always been, the only avenue by which a sinner can obtain salvation. "No man cometh unto the Father, but by me."

It is reported that when the *Titanic* was sinking, a millionaire came to a man sitting in one of the lifeboats, which was about to be lowered, and offered him one hundred thousand dollars for his place in the boat. The man in the boat refused. The scarcity of places made the value of one priceless. The only avenue of escape was the lifeboat. Christ is the only lifeboat that can be launched from a doomed and sinking world, and his blood buys the only seat in the lifeboat. He pays the price and offers it to any lost sinner who will take it. It costs the sinner nothing, but it cost him everything. The blood of Christ alone suffices to purchase redemption for the sinner. It alone has merit before God. It opens the gate of heaven and lets the sinner in. It is the subject of every song in heaven. It is the latest song in heaven.

"What can wash away my sin?
Nothing but the blood of Jesus."
—*Robert Lowry*

CHAPTER 16

Bought and Paid For

"In whom we have redemption through his blood, the forgiveness of sins, according to the riches of his grace" (Ephesians 1:7). Redemption is one of the high terms of salvation. It is sometimes used to connote the entire field of Christology, as in Strong's *Theology*. In its broader sense, it speaks of the person and work of Christ. However, it is a more inclusive term than that, and there is danger of it losing its technical meaning if given such a broad application. It requires a restriction to keep it in proper bounds. This can be attained when redemption is kept related to the Hebrew *goel*, as we have previously indicated. When so restricted, it is as Wilkes declares: "There is no theme so solemn and yet so blessed as that of redemption." Redemption means "to purchase by paying a price." In the case of the sinner, the price is the blood of Christ. Redemption has been defined as: "The act of Deity in which Jesus Christ pays the whole demand of the law against the sinner, redeeming him from the curse and bondage of the law: the Father receives him as son and heir, and the Holy Spirit delivers him from the bondage to indwelling sin."

Redemption is postulated on the fact of sin. If sin does not exist, then redemption is a useless work and a meaningless word. The entire plan of redemption rests upon the reality of sin. Therefore the reality of sin must be established as actually existing in the life of the race. It must be demonstrated that sin is something over which man has no power. The redeemer is made necessary because man is helpless in the presence of sin.

First, we wish to discuss the fact of sin. When man sinned in the Garden of Eden, God put this question to Eve: "What is this that thou hast done" (Genesis 3:13)? It was a question that neither the man nor the woman could answer adequately. This moot question is only handled satisfactorily in the New Testament. It is possible for us to get an adequate conception of sin. Tholuck, in his address celebrating the fiftieth anniversary of his professorship at Halle, made this poignant statement: "In review of God's manifold blessings, the thing I seem most to thank him for is the conviction of sin." God's revelation concerning sin, and six thousand years of human history give some conception of the "exceeding sinfulness of sin."

There is no excuse for feeble ideas about the sin problem. Liberal theology in America has entertained light notions about sin during the entire history of our Republic. This psychological religion has called man "a momentary figure in the dance of the atoms." Sin is described as a "relic of the theological jungle." Sin has been outmoded, according to some. Dr. Shaler Matthews defines sin as "the backward pull of an outworn good." In other words, there was a time when sin was good. It at least has a good background, according to this definition. The light of revelation and history will not yield to these feeble notions.

A full-orbed conception of sin is presented to us, and sin can be seen in its effect upon man and upon God. First, let us see the effect of sin upon man. This is revealed in a threefold manner:

1. *The Extent of Sin.*

"For there is no man that sinneth not" (I Kings 8:46). Sin extends out to each member of the human family. No individual has escaped the corruption of sin. This is another way of saying that sin is universal. No member of the race is immune to it, nor is it possible to get inoculated against it. Cancer is a dreadful and dreaded disease, yet very few of the race, comparatively speaking, suffer from it. Poverty is a terrible existence, yet some have escaped its meshes. But sin is far-reaching in its consequences, for it has touched each member of the race. Every baby born into the race inherits a sinful nature. Men are sinners by birth, and by act. Where the revelation of God's Word has gone, men have been made aware of this. Goethe said, "I see no fault committed which I too might not have committed." Dr. Johnson commented, "Every man knows that of himself which he dares not tell to his dearest friends"; and Count de Maistre said, "I do not know what the heart of a villain may be—I only know that of a virtuous man, and that is frightful." The novelist Thackeray has no heroes as paragons of virtue to cross the pages of his novels, and George Eliot has all of her characters act from mixed motives. They were attempting to picture human nature accurately. Some men have declared that they live free from sin, but the facts of their lives have proven otherwise. Rousseau, in his *Confessions,* uttered a prayer in which he said, "Eternal Spirit, the soul that I am going to give thee back is as pure at this moment as it was when it proceeded from thee." Yet virtually all, if not all, of his children were illegitimate, and he sent them all off to a foundling hospital.

All of these corroborate the assertion of Scripture: "All have sinned, and come short of the glory of God" (Romans 3:23).

2. *The Intent of Sin.*

It is the full intention of sin to destroy the entire race. It is fully capable of doing just that. Sin is responsible for every heartache, pain, grey hair, stoop in the shoulder, totter in the step, wrecked life and broken home; and, finally, it will bring death, for "the wages of sin is death." The practice of sin is fatal to man.

3. *The Content of Sin.*

Sin has within it that element which makes it utterly impossible for man to cope with it. Man has no remedy which he can concoct for sin. He cannot close Pandora's box. If it were possible for him to get rid of sin, would it not be sensible for the whole race to get up some morning, bright and early, eat a hearty breakfast, and then set out in dead earnest to drive it from the universe by sunset? Man could not do this in a day nor in an eternity.

The effect of sin upon God reveals something of a far-reaching nature. Sin has hung the crepe on the door of heaven. It has wounded the heart of God, marred his creation, and intruded into his very presence. The effect of sin upon God will likewise be treated under a threefold division:

1. Sin Has Caused God to Lose His Fellowship with Man (temporarily at least).

God created man for fellowship and came down to enjoy that relationship with Adam. It can be said reverently that on the afternoon in which Adam ran away, God was lonesome. There is no way for us to measure the yearning in the heart of God for that man. Sin disrupted the relationship in such a way that man's state makes it impossible for God to see any merit in him that might be offered to make amends.

2. Sin Has Caused God to Punish the Sinner.

There was no other alternative; the sinner must die. God banished Adam from the Garden and imputed sin to all his posterity. The race from Adam stood guilty before God, and deserved the death penalty. All this brought anguish to the heart of God, for it is "not his will that any should perish." "As I live, saith the Lord God, I have no pleasure in the death of the wicked" (Ezekiel 33:11). This does not mean that God apologizes for punishing sin. On the other hand, he declares freely that

171

he will punish it, for it not only is contrary to his nature, but it is rebellion against his character. Of him it is declared: "He doth judge and make war."

3. The Presence of Sin Prompted God to Make the Supreme Sacrifice to Redeem the Sinner.

To know something about the depths of sin, it is necessary to stand at the cross. The suffering of Christ attests the heinousness of sin, although it is beyond the ability of man fully to evaluate the extent of his passion. Man can stand at the foot of the cross in awe and say with the apostle, "He was made sin for us." The cross is God's answer to the sin question. It is not a question now, in the light of the cross, of why he permitted sin to enter the universe. But the inscrutable mystery now is: Why did he pay such a price for the sinner? The answer is hushed in the heart of God. Jerusalem never knew the meaning of the cross he bore through her streets and out through her gate, and even the New Jerusalem will only be able to sing:

"Amazing grace! how sweet the sound,
That saved a wretch like me!
I once was lost, but now am found,
Was blind, but now I see."

Sin is a flagrant insult against God, for which man is guilty and over which he has no power. Redemption is the answer of God to the presence of sin. Sometimes the question is asked, "Why did God permit sin?" There is another question which is parallel to it and which must be asked at the same time, if fairness is intended to God in this matter:

172

"Why did God permit redemption?" The answer to the second question is found in the first question. Immediately, at the first appearance of sin, God was there developing the doctrine of redemption, and making it available for sinners. We wish now to follow the development of the doctrine of redemption in Scripture from the Old Testament into the New.

At first, redemption meant deliverance from any calamity that might befall one in this life. "The Angel which redeemed me from all evil, bless the lads; and let my name be named on them, and the name of my fathers Abraham and Isaac; and let them grow into a multitude in the midst of the earth" (Genesis 48:16). Jacob recognized, in his old age, that he had been kept from evil by a power greater than himself. His innate tendency, as his history demonstrates, was an inclination to sin. The angel of God had kept him from evil, and in this sense he had been redeemed from it. He was delivered from evil, which was a redemption on the human plane. Eliphaz spoke of a redemption from death in the time of famine, and of a deliverance from the sword in time of war. "In famine he shall redeem thee from death: and in war from the power of the sword" (Job 5:20).

Job spoke of a redemption from the hand of the enemy. "Or, Deliver me from the enemy's hand? or, Redeem me from the hand of the mighty?" (Job 6:23).

Anyone could act as redeemer in these matters of this life. However, there was a strong insistence that God was the redeemer, in the deliverance from

173

the bondage of Egypt. Although Moses was the human instrument used, it was Jehovah who declared: "I will bring you out from under the burdens of the Egyptians, and I will rid you out of their bondage, and I will redeem you with a stretched-out arm, and with great judgments" (Exodus 6:6). Moses had a rod in his hand that he used, but he was the rod in God's hand. It was God who intervened when Israel was hopelessly shackled in the chains of Egypt. After the deliverance from Egypt, God was called the Redeemer of Israel. Psalm seventy-eight, which recounts the Egyptian episode, speaks of God in this way: "And they remembered that God was their rock, and the high God their redeemer" (verse 35). The Prophet Isaiah used the title "Redeemer" more times than it occurs in the remainder of the Bible. It was a term used exclusively of Jehovah in the prophet's time. "Thou shalt also suck the milk of the Gentiles, and shalt suck the breast of kings: and thou shalt know that I the Lord am thy Saviour and thy Redeemer [*Goel*], the mighty One of Jacob" (Isaiah 60:16).

Finally, redemption applied specifically to the deliverance of the soul from sin; and as the term became restricted to this, God alone became the redeemer. By the time of the kingdom, it was revealed that God alone could act in the capacity of a redeemer from sin. "None of them can by any means redeem his brother, nor give to God a ransom for him: (for the redemption of their soul is precious, and it ceaseth forever)" (Psalm 49:7,8). The explanation of why man could not redeem his brother is found in the further statement: "But God will redeem my soul from the power of the grave" (verse 15). The full-flowered development of the doctrine of redemption in the Old Testament is made by one of the pre-exilic prophets. "I will ransom them from the power of the grave; I will redeem them from death: O death, I will be thy plagues; O grave, I will be thy destruction: repentance shall be hid from mine eyes" (Hosea 13:14). This is a prophecy that reaches on into the kingdom for its final fulfillment. It found a partial and basic fulfillment in the resurrection of Christ, and Paul so interprets it in the fifteenth chapter of First Corinthians. However, the important feature here is that Jehovah is seen in his unique position of a redeemer from sin. A redemption from the grave and death was to the Hebrew a redemption from sin.

It is not until we come to the New Testament that we find the doctrine of redemption fully developed. Here it is restricted to the deliverance purchased by the Redeemer on behalf of the sinner in the payment of the penalty of sin. The blood of Christ was the medium of exchange used to make this tremendous transaction. Redemption in the New Testament is a progressive work based upon the redemptive act of the shedding of Christ's blood. The blood is the basis for the redemptive work of God. Redemption is, first of all, a deliverance from the *penalty* of sin. This was accomplished by Christ shedding his blood on the cross. In the next place, redemption is a deliverance from the *power* of sin. This is accomplished by the indwelling Holy Spirit. Finally, redemption is a deliverance from the *presence* of sin. This will be accomplished by the *parousia* of Christ. Paul made this threefold division of the redemption made by Christ: "Who delivered us from so great a death, and doth deliver: in whom we trust that he will yet deliver us" (II Corinthians 1:10).

The death of Christ accomplished one great thing: namely, the salvation of man. But in its relationship to time, it touches all phases of man's life. It is past, present and future. It moves out of time and reaches back into eternity past where it was in the mind of God, and found the basis of the covenant in the Godhead of redemption. It reaches forth into the future and lays hold of eternity to come where in anticipation the redeemed are seen in heaven. There are some Greek words which are translated by our word, *redeem*, but each one of these conveys the thought as expressed in one of the time periods. (1) *Agorazo* refers to the past. (2) *Exagorazo* refers to the present. (3) *Lutroo* or *apolutrosis* refers to the future. We shall now take occasion to examine each one of these phases of redemption as they are related to the saved today.

1. Redemption is a Deliverance from the Penalty of Sin.

This has particular reference to the redemption purchased by Christ through the shedding of his own blood on the cross. The blood of Christ is full payment for sin. It is an account settled in the past. The question of the penalty of sin for the redeemed will never be raised again in this life or eternity. "Verily, verily, I say unto you, He that heareth my word, and believeth on him that sent me, hath everlasting life, and shall not come into condemnation [judgment]; but is passed from death unto life" (John 5:24). This phase of redemption is seen in the meaning and use of the first word which is translated redeem, *agorazo*. This word means "to do business in the market place," such as buying and selling. This word suggests the Oriental agora where everything was displayed for sale, including human beings. Slaves were as common there as any vegetable or meat. Gibbon, in the *Decline and Fall of the Roman Empire,* estimates that at least one-half of the population of the Roman Empire were slaves. This means that about sixty million people were slaves. Human life was cheap, and the traffic in it was tremendous. Both Gibbon and John Lord give slavery as one of the basic reasons for the undermining and corruption of the Roman Empire, and which, ultimately, led to its downfall.

The New Testament, written in these surroundings, sees man as a slave to sin. The whole human family is in the shackles of sin, and in dire need of a redeemer. Paul speaks of himself in inspired language: "I am carnal, sold under sin" (Romans 7:14). This is a miniature picture of the race. Again, he. tells the Ephesians of their condition before deliverance was wrought. "Wherein in time past ye walked according to the course of this world, according to the prince of the power of the air, the spirit that now worketh in the children of disobedience" (Ephesians 2:2). They were slaves of sin, and because of that, they did the will of Satan. This does not even suggest that Satan was the owner who had slaves exposed in the market place for sale. This would mean that Christ paid the ransom

177

to the devil. This is not the intent of the apostle. Nowhere does Scripture intimate that the redemptive price paid by Christ, even his own blood, was to the devil.

The patristic theory of the Atonement, or the military theory of the Atonement, as it has been popularly labeled, taught that sinners were held as captives of war by Satan, and that they could be bought by a ransom paid to him. Justin Martyr was the perpetrator of this theory, and it was taken up by Irenaeus and Origen. It may be briefly stated in the words of Peter Lombard: "What did the Redeemer to our captor? He held out to him his cross as a mouse-trap; in it he set, as a bait, his blood." This heresy was also called the "mouse-trap" theory. Accordingly, Christ paid a ransom to Satan with His blood. This appears to us highly preposterous and blasphemous, but the theory was held by many able men in the church during its early history; and today there are some who border on this theory, even if they do not embrace it.

Anselm in the eleventh century was the first to successfully refute this heresy. He pointed out that whatever man owed, he owed to God and not to Satan. Man cannot render any payment to God because of original sin, or as he stated, "A sinner cannot justify a sinner." Only God could satisfy the claims of God. Therefore, as he further stated: "If then none can make it but God, and none owes it but man, it must needs be wrought out by God, made man."

Satan is a usurper here in the world, and man owes nothing to him. God does not recognize as an eternal matter his claims to this earth, but treats him as a rebel who temporarily has overthrown man's dominion by a *coup d'etat* in the universe of God, and usurped God's authority. Christ's death was not an overture to Satan, and certainly Christ was making no payment to him. Christ did not buy us from Satan, but he did redeem us from the penalty of sin and the power of Satan. We no longer have to serve the usurper. In *Cur Deus Homo*, Anselm makes the death of Christ and the shedding of his blood a transaction entirely in the Godhead. Paul stated it thus: "God was in Christ, reconciling the world unto himself." The price was made to satisfy the demands of his own holiness.

Philip Mauro, it seems to us, has fallen into the error of the military theory of the Atonement. We quote at length from him that we might have his exact language. In commenting on Leviticus 25:47-49 he writes: "For men, instead of occupying in the world that place of dominion and supreme authority for which God intended them, have become slaves to a foreign despot, namely, that great being who has 'the power of death, that is, the devil' (Hebrews 2:14); and have become subject to 'the law of sin and death' (Romans 8:2). For we may regard the devil as being that 'stranger' to whom the human race has been sold by the head of the race (Adam) and 'the stock of the stranger's family' to be the evil powers, vices and passions, by which men are, one and all, enslaved."

The stranger in the Leviticus passage, which we have examined beforehand, could not be Satan. Christ did not pay one iota to Satan. The stranger was the one who received the price of redemption; and it is a dangerous practice to make him a figure of Satan. Christ paid the penalty of sin to satisfy the justice of God so that we might not have to pay it. Sin, not Satan, prompted Christ to go into the market place and ransom us from the penalty of it. The sacrifice of Christ was not satisfactory to Satan. Satan was not a party in the transaction of redemption.

Christ died a penal death. He went into the market place and saw us exposed as slaves of sin. In such a condition, we were subject to death. Christ paid the price of the penalty of our sin, and lifted the terrible load of sin that was on the slave's back.

2. Redemption is a Deliverance from the Power of Sin.

The entire plan of redemption rests upon the foundation of the death of Christ. In view of this, the Holy Spirit came on the day of Pentecost to make this phase of redemption available to man. Not only is the sinner delivered from the penalty of sin, but he can be delivered from the power of sin in this life. There is a way. This has to do with the everyday walk of the believer. The Greek word which applies particularly to this phase of *exagorazo*.

Liddell and Scott give the meaning "to buy from" and "to redeem." It is the same word that occurs under (1), but with the addition of the preposition EK, meaning "out of." It means, therefore, "to buy out of the market place." Dr. Scofield, who has called attention to this threefold division, makes this enlightening comment: "Our adorable Kinsman-Redeemer is no slave trader." He not only bought us in the market place of sin, that shameful Oriental bazaar; but he took us off the market so that we might never be sold again. There is no danger of the redeemed sinner ever going on the slave block again. This refers to the security of redemption because it makes it possible for a sinning saint to come back to God and find power, never to fall again into the same heinous sin. John expressed it in this way: "But if we walk in the light, as he is in the light, we have fellowship one with another, and the blood of Jesus Christ his Son cleanseth us from all sin" (I John 1:7).

The present tense is used here in reference to the cleansing of the blood of Christ. That it keeps on cleansing us from all sin is the thought. This refers to the present walk of the believer here on earth. There is redemption from the power of sin in the daily life.

The Holy Spirit furnishes deliverance from the power of present sin. If the Christian is not producing the fruit of the Spirit, he is doing the works of the flesh. There is no no such thing as a "no-man's land" in between. The works of the flesh are sin, and are so identified in the Word of God. "For I know that in me (that is, in my flesh) dwelleth no good thing."

If a Christian produces no fruit of the Spirit, but lives in the flesh, can he expect to be saved? This is a pertinent question that baffles, because a great many "so-called" Christians are living in the flesh. If it is admitted that these "so-called" Christians have been redeemed by the blood of the Lamb, then we may dismiss any question regarding the certainty of their salvation. They are saved. If they have not been redeemed from the penalty of sin, then they cannot figure in the discussion under this section. They have not been delivered from the penalty of sin. They need to accept the redemption that is offered by grace, if they but trust Christ. In this section, we are discussing genuine Christians who have been redeemed by the blood of the Lamb. We are not considering their future redemption and eternal welfare; but we are confined in our discussion to the narrow limits of their present lives. How a Christian may be delivered from the power of sin right *now* is the cogent question before us. Does God have a present redemption available for saved sinners by which they can live for him?

This is peculiarly the age of the Holy Spirit. His most peculiar ministry, which is in contrast to other ages, is that he indwells every believer. "But ye are not in the flesh, but in the Spirit, if so be that the Spirit of God dwell in you. Now if any man have not the Spirit of Christ, he is none of his" (Romans 8:9). "What? know ye not that your body is the temple of the Holy Ghost which is in you, which ye have of God, and ye are not your own" (I Corinthians 6:19)?

The indwelling of believers is the grand indentification of this age. The day of Pentecost marks the transition from the Old Testament, where the Holy Spirit came and went in a sovereign way, to the New Testament where he has come on a specific ministry. One phase of this ministry is to indwell believers. The day of Pentecost was the line of demarcation between the Old and New, law and grace, and Israel and the Church.

Pentecost was the Bethlehem of the Holy Spirit. He came to dwell in the body of believers on that day. To read over the day of Pentecost as an incident in the development of the gospel story is to miss the significance and import of the tremendous transaction of that day. There was a difference after Pentecost. There would have been no Church, no evangel, no testimony, no epistles and no Apostle Paul if there had not been that day. Christ carefully instructed his disciples to abide in Jerusalem after his ascension: "But ye shall receive power, after that the Holy Ghost is come upon you: and ye shall be witnesses unto me." He warned them that "they should not depart from Jerusalem, but wait for the promise of the Father." The Church was born in Jerusalem. The New Jerusalem had its inception in the earthly city, but Jerusalem was not long to be the center of the Christian movement, for it was soon shifted to the Gentile city of Antioch, and from there to the four corners of the earth.

Ten days after the ascension of Christ, the disciples were gathered together in some place. Was it the upper room, the Temple, or some other place? They had just had an election of an apostle to take Judas' place, conducted by the incomparable but "wrong-way" Simon Peter. This election proved that they needed divine light and leading. Perhaps Matthias was a devout and faithful saint in Christ Jesus, but the Holy Spirit was not there to choose him as an apostle, and apparently did not use him in that capacity afterwards. Then the Holy Spirit came. There was no star, no angel voices, and no wise men, but his advent was marked by tangible and vital evidence. There were two evidences that he had come. First of all, there was a "sound from heaven as of a rushing mighty wind." It was not a wind, but that was the effect produced; that was what the witnesses heard. Secondly, there were "cloven tongues like as of fire." It was not fire, but that was the effect produced; that was what the witnesses saw.

There are two avenues through which man comes into possession of most of his knowledge. One is the eye gate and the other is the ear gate. The Holy Spirit confirmed his entrance into the believers by an appeal to both. He revealed his presence by sight and sound. Those present both saw and heard. That day was never repeated in the life of the Church, for the Holy Spirit came to indwell. There is no necessity for a repetition as he is already here; and he will not come again because he has not left since the day of Pentecost. As long as the Church is here, he will be here.

He indwells every believer and is the power for Christian living. Christian living is permitting him to work through the life. This was never true under the Old Testament arrangement. The ideal of Christian living is, therefore, much higher than that under law. "Rejoice evermore" was not a commandment under law but is a production of the indwelling Holy Spirit in the life of a Spirit-filled child of God. The great commandment for the age of grace is: "Be filled with the Spirit" or "Walk in the Spirit."

Christian living is not keeping law or following some scheme of conduct. It might be possible for a Christian to keep certain laws and rules which would make him feel as though he were doing a good job of Christian living when in reality he would be making a horrible mess of it. Christian living is yielding to the operation of the Holy Spirit in order that he may produce "the fruit of the Spirit."

Just as a peach tree yields itself to the sweet influence of the sun, rain and gentle breezes, so the Christian is to yield to the Holy Spirit. Just as the peach tree produces sweet fruit as it yields, thus the Christian will produce the fruit of the Spirit. This fruit is not an unknown quantity but is distinctly outlined: "Love, joy, peace, longsuffering, gentleness, goodness, faith, meekness, temperance: against such there is no law" (Galatians 5:22,23).

These graces cannot be produced by human effort or resolution but are distinctly declared to be fruit. A peach is not the product of the effort of the peach tree, but represents what a power greater than the peach tree can produce. A Christian may know, by examining his own life, if these things are being produced. If these things are absent from the life of the Christian, he is falling short of God's ideal for him. His salvation is secure, but he is missing the blessing of living for God and the prospect of a future reward.

The Holy Spirit is the power for Christian living today. When our great Redeemer bought us in the market place of sin, he led us out from under the power of sin and bade us live by the new power that he had provided for us. He does not wish to sell us back under sin, but has led us out from the old life. We have been redeemed from the law to the new life under grace.

3. Redemption is a Deliverance from the Presence of Sin.

"Christ being come an high priest of good things to come ... entered in once into the holy place, having obtained eternal redemption for us" (Hebrews 9:11,12).

The final word, which is before us, is from a different origin than the other two. It is the Greek word *lutroo*, and the form *apolutrosis*, which occurs in the noun form. The preposition does not add anything to the meaning of this word, but merely intensifies it. Both words mean "to release by payment of ransom." Simply stated, they mean "to set free." "As our Kinsman-Redeemer is no slave trader, so also, he is not a slave owner." The slave has not only been removed from the slave block forever, but he has been removed from the position of slave. He has been removed that he might be set free. Redemption is the "Proclamation of Emancipation" for sinners, written in the blood of Christ. "If the Son therefore shall make you free, ye shall be free indeed" (John 8:36). "For, brethren, ye have been called unto liberty; only use not liberty for an occasion to the flesh, but by love serve one another" (Galatians 5:13).

Redemption removes a sinner from the death cell, and brings him into the Father's house and establishes him in the position of sonship. "For ye have not received the spirit of bondage again to

186

fear; but ye have received the Spirit of adoption, whereby we cry, Abba, Father" (Romans 8:15). Redemption removes a sinner from the death cell and eventually sees the sinner at last delivered from the presence of sin and brought into the presence of God. Christ is the one who brings us all the way. He is our redemption, for he "is made unto us ... redemption." Twice over we are told: "In whom we have redemption through his blood" (Ephesians 1:7; Colossians 1:14). This word, therefore, deals definitely with the future aspect of redemption. Sin will be removed from the presence of the redeemed, and from this earth. There are two features of future redemption which must await the coming of Christ before they can be fulfilled. These are: the redemption of our bodies and the redemption of creation.

Paul speaks of the redemption of the body as future. "And not only they, but ourselves also, which have the firstfruits of the Spirit, even we ourselves groan within ourselves, waiting for the adoption, to wit, the redemption of our body" (Romans 8:23). We will not be completely redeemed until we have a body redeemed from sin and death. Although the redeemed are, at present, indwelt by the Holy Spirit, they do not have a body which is delivered from sin and death. The old Adamic nature lives on until death, or until Christ translates the living believers. The resurrection of believers comprehends a new body. "For this corruptible must put on incorruption, and this mortal must put on immortality" (I Corinthians 15:53). This old Adamic, dying body "is sown in corruption; it is raised in incorruption." The modern method is to diffuse the physical resurrection of the body into thin air by substituting for the Christian doctrine of resurrection the Buddhist and Platonic philosophies, which deny the actual resurrection of the body by making it spiritual. Paul defended the Christian doctrine against that very system when he wrote: "It is sown a natural body; it is raised a spiritual body. There is a natural body, and there is a spiritual body" (I Corinthians 15:44).

The body will be retained in resurrection. Instead of having a body dominated by the fallen, Adamic nature, we will possess a body dominated by the Spirit of God, and motivated by the Spirit of God breathed anew into it. It is impossible to dismiss the resurrection of the body from the Christian doctrine. Redemption will not be complete until the bodies of the redeemed are raised in newness of life. Paul contemplated that day when he wrote: "And grieve not the holy Spirit of God, whereby ye are sealed unto the day of redemption" (Ephesians 4:30). The "day of redemption," here mentioned, is the time of the resurrection of the saints who have died, and the translation of the living saints at the *parousia* of Christ.

The second prospect of future redemption is the lifting of the curse from physical creation. When Adam sinned, there was a curse pronounced upon the earth: "Cursed is the ground for thy sake; in sorrow shalt thou eat of it all the days of thy life; thorns also and thistles shall it bring forth to thee" (Genesis 3:17,18). "A blasted earth" fittingly describes the continued condition of our planet down to the present hour, a phenomenon Paul recognizes in Romans eight. "The whole creation groaneth and travaileth in pain together until now."

The poet may speak of communing with nature and of the sweetness of that process; but the farmer who has wrestled with Johnson grass and cockleburs in fertile bottom land in the afternoon of a hot, sultry July day does not call it communion, nor does he find any particular sweetness in it. The earth does not respond readily to the efforts of man, but it must be compelled, by persistent effort, to yield her increase. Only by the "sweat of the brow" does man eke out a living from the ground. Still, there are times when the earth overcomes the handicap of the curse and yields bountifully, filling her cornucopia to overflowing. It is, however, a figment of the imagination and an oratorical gesture to say that man has conquered the forces of nature and has made them subservient to his beck and call.

There is a golden day in the future for this earth, for the one who created it will be here to make nature respond with her hidden treasures and possibilities, as he did when he made the fish bring a coin to Simon Peter in order for him to pay the Temple tax. The curse will be lifted from the earth during the millennium; and then man will have his first glimpse of this planet in her original beauty. The mind cannot conceive of the desert rejoicing and blossoming as the rose, yet this is the happy anticipation of the earth.

If it were possible for man today to bring in the kingdom of heaven on the earth, which is the modern delusion of the church, this important task of restoring the fecundity of the earth and lifting the curse would be a difficulty that even the most optimistic "kingdom-builder" could not handle. The many improvements which man has made are no substitute for the ideal conditions outlined in Scripture. At present, many Bible students, filled with zeal and ardor, are speaking with rapture of the wonders that the returning Jews have wrought in Palestine by modern methods of farming. They imply that this is, at least, a partial fulfillment of Scripture. These changes, however, are hardly commensurate with what is spoken in Isaiah 11:6-8; 30:26; and 35. The entire face of the earth will be transformed into a scene of placid beauty and verdant landscape.

Christ is the great kinsman-redeemer who will deliver the bodies of believers in a physical resurrection, and will deliver the physical creation from the bondage of the curse. Boaz delivered both the person of Ruth and the property of Elimelech. Christ will deliver the person of the Church and the property of the Jew and Gentile, which is this earth. Future redemption contemplates the resurrection of redeemed persons and the restoration of a sin-cursed earth. Then there will be freedom.

There may be some objection to the inclusion of a love story like Ruth in the canon of Scripture. This objection may be intensified when it is concluded that the Book of Ruth teaches the great doctrine of redemption by a kinsman-redeemer. Nevertheless, the story stands, and the fact remains that redemption is a love story. It was the love of our Kinsman-Redeemer, as he saw us plunged in the slavery of sin, that prompted him to pay with his own blood the price of our release, and he has brought us into his house and heart because he loved us.

BIBLIOGRAPHY

(Those works which are marked with an asterisk
have proved particularly valuable and helpful.)

COMMENTARIES

*Grant. *The Numerical Bible*. Vol. II, pp. 268-283. New York: Loizeaux Bros., 1894.

Gaebelein, A. C. *The Annotated Bible*. Vol. II, pp. 117-125. New York: "Our Hope" Publication, 1915.

Jamieson, Fausset, and Brown. pp. 173-175. *Commentary on the Old and New Testaments*. Grand Rapids: Zondervan Publishing House.

Kiel and Delitzsch. *Biblical Commentary on the Old Testament*, Vol. IV, pp. 465-494. Edinburgh: T. and T. Clark, 1865.

GENERAL

Calvin, John. *The Institutes of The Christian Religion*. pp. 305-312. Philadelphia: Westminster Press.

Chafer, L. S. *Grace*. pp. 1-357. Grand Rapids: Zondervan Publishing House.

Gaebelein, A. C. *Gospel of Matthew*. pp. 25-27. Neptune, N.J.: Loizeaux Bros.

Lee, Robert. *The Outlined Bible*. Anaylsis No. 8. Glasgow: Pickering and Inglis.

Mauro, Philip. *Ruth, The Satisfied Stranger*. pp. 1-220. Swangel, Pa.: Reiner Publishing.

*Moorhouse, Henry. *Ruth, The Moabitess*. pp. 1-66. New York: F. H. Revell, 1881.

Noble, F. A. *Our Redemption, Its Need, Method and Result*. pp. 1-282. New York: Fleming H. Revell Co., 1897.

Putnam, C. E. *The Power of Jesus' Blood and Its Relation to Sin*. pp. 3-64. Chicago: Bible Institute Colportage Association, 1920.

Strong, A. H. *Systematic Theology*. pp. 665-773, 573-582. Philadelphia: The Judson Press.